THE PARACHUTE REGIMENT

The Parachute Regiment is the airborne infantry of the British Army and has been at the forefront of operations since it was raised in World War Two. Distinctive in their coveted red berets, these soldiers have a proven combat pedigree and developed a military brand which is world renowned. The regiment is shaped to deliver operations by parachute, air-landed by transport aircraft, or helicopter. It can project power, deliver influence, and reinforce political intent with the 'military force' poised at a forward mounting base or deployed in the air ready to intervene. Today, the Paras include four battalions and operates as part of 16 Air Assault Brigade Combat Team (16AABCT) delivering the airborne manoeuvre capability of the UK's new Global Response Force (GRF), with a joint-force capability with the American 82nd Airborne Division.

Airborne forces emerged after the fall of France in May 1940, when Prime Minister Winston Churchill was eager to create a new fighting force that could strike at enemy-occupied Europe. Among the troops he had in mind were parachute forces, which he was aware had been used to great effect by the Nazis to seize key objectives. These coups de main operations, which the War Office had previously dismissed, had attracted his attention and he called for more information about this new military development.

Churchill soon decided that Britain should raise its own capability and called for a force of at least 5,000 parachute troops. By the end of the war the Parachute Regiment

had swelled to 17 battalions and had seen action in France , Sicily, Greece, and North Africa, where General Rommel's forces dubbed the Paras, the 'Red Devils'. The regiment spearheaded the invasion of Europe on June 6, 1944, dropping into Normandy to secure bridges ahead of the amphibious assault. They fought with courage in September of the same year when the 1st Airborne Division, alongside American and Polish troops, dropped into Holland.

At Arnhem, ground forces were delayed in linking up with them, leaving the Paras to face overwhelming German forces in a mission that became known as a 'Bridge Too Far'. In the post war-years they were sent into Palestine, across the Middle East, and the jungles of Malaya. Then, when the Egyptian government seized control of the Suez Canal from the British and French owned company that managed it, a combined force from the UK and France parachuted into El Gamil in 1956. The regiment then served on internal security duty in Aden and Northern Ireland. When Argentina invaded the Falkland Islands in April 1982, the Paras were in the vanguard of the action again. They took part in the Invasion of Iraq and were the first into Afghanistan in 2001 and last out in 2021.

The Parachute Regiment is held at high-readiness to deploy anywhere across the globe on warfighting, intervention, and rescue missions. In an uncertain world of global instability, the regiment provides the UK government with an immediate military capability and has a close bond with American and French airborne forces regularly taking part in joint deployments across Europe in a relationship which has evolved through operational collaboration. On operations the Parachute Regiment's core means of insertion is by parachute. The RAF's Airbus A400M is the modern-day workhouse of the force, replacing the C-130J Hercules, designed to ferry paratroopers to their objective. Pilots are trained to approach the drop zone at low level to avoid enemy radar and surface-to-air missile systems. Then, as they approach the drop zone they gain altitude – releasing their paratroopers from just 450 feet. They use the Irvin Low Level parachute, a dynamic canopy that has been in service for more than 20 years. Today, the regiment stands as their motto states , 'Ready for Anything'.

King Charles III is the colonel-in-chief of the Parachute Regiment having been appointed to the role in 1977. In 1978 as the Prince of Wales he underwent the parachute training course at RAF Brize Norton in order that he could look soldiers who wore the red beret 'in the eye' when wearing the infamous red beret.

David Reynolds Editor

CONTENTS

(MOD/Ministry of Defence)

(MOD/Ministry of Defence)

Its objective was to push 60 miles into German territory with a bridgehead over the Lower Rhine River, creating an Allied invasion route into northern Germany. Two American divisions and one British, the 1st Airborne Division, were assigned to the task which would see a carpet of paratroopers dropped into Holland.

76 Post War Operations

The Parachute Regiment mounted its first post-war operational jump in 1956 into Egypt, after politicians had resorted to military action following the nationalisation of the Franco-British Suez Canal Company by Colonel Gamal Abdel Nasser. He believed that in only five years the tolls collected from ships passing through the Suez Canal would pay for the construction of the Aswan Dam. Nasser's actions were seen as a threat to both British and French interests in the region.

86 Ready For Anything

Since 1969 the Parachute Regiment had been deployed in Northern Ireland on internal security operations. Then in early 1982 as the 1st battalion remained on duty on the streets of Belfast, both the 2nd and 3rd battalions found themselves being recalled from leave and sent 8,000 miles to the South Atlantic as part of a British Task Force to eject Argentinian forces from the Falklands. Here the regiment fought with distinction at Goose Green and Mount Longdon and won two Victoria Crosses for valour.

98 Evacuation in Sierra Leone

In 2000, the Parachute Regiment spearheaded an evacuation in Sierra Leone, codenamed Operation Palliser. The Revolutionary United Front (RUF) was locked in a bloody civil war with government forces and had committed barbaric acts of violence, including mutilating civilians in order to prevent them voting in future elections. As they moved towards the capital, Downing Street approved the evacuation amid concerns for the safety of British nationals and diplomats based there.

108 Afghanistan

The Parachute Regiment was among the first units to deploy to Afghanistan, following the terrorist attacks on the United States in September 2001. The 2nd battalion arrived in Kabul in late 2001 tasked with establishing NATO's International Security Assistance Force (ISAF). Later, the regiment was called on to spearhead a 'break in battle' into Helmand in the south of the country and then in 2021 was sent back in to spearhead the biggest evacuation of civilians since World War Two.

ISBN: 9781802829501
Editor: David Reynolds
Senior editor, specials: Roger Mortimer
Email: roger.mortimer@keypublishing.com
Cover Design: Steve Donovan
Design: SJmagic DESIGN SERVICES, India
Advertising Sales Manager: Sam Clark
Email: sam.clark@keypublishing.com
Tel: 01780 755131
Advertising Production:
Becky Antoniades
Email: Rebecca.antoniades@keypublishing.com

SUBSCRIPTION/MAIL ORDER
Key Publishing Ltd, PO Box 300, Stamford,
Lincs, PE9 1NA
Tel: 01780 480404
Subscriptions email:
subs@keypublishing.com

Mail Order email: orders@keypublishing.com
Website: www.keypublishing.com/shop

PUBLISHING
Group CEO and Publisher: Adrian Cox
Published by
Key Publishing Ltd, PO Box 100, Stamford,
Lincs, PE9 1XQ
Tel: 01780 755131
Website: www.keypublishing.com

PRINTING
Precision Colour Printing Ltd, Haldane,
Halesfield 1, Telford, Shropshire. TF7 4QQ

DISTRIBUTION
Seymour Distribution Ltd, 2 Poultry Avenue,
London, EC1A 9PU
Enquiries Line: 02074 294000.

The Global Response Force was formed to provide the UK with an immediate military response to unforeseen global events. (DPL)

GLOBAL RESPONSE FORCE

As a core element of the UK's new **Global Response Force (GRF)**, the Parachute Regiment maintains an 'on call' rapid response with units permanently at high readiness for worldwide intervention operations. As part of 16 Air Assault Brigade Combat Team (16AABCT) the Parachute Regiment's soldiers are trained to conduct a range of missions, from prevention and pre-emption tasks, to complex, high intensity war-fighting. The brigade has close links with its American airborne counterparts, taking part in regular training together and maintains a strategic 'joint-capability' to deliver 'long range parachute insertion' across the globe.

The Global Response Force was formed to provide the UK with an immediate military response to unforeseen global events. The Paras had a major role in the previous Joint Rapid Reaction Force (JRRF) which was formed in 1999. After enduring operations in Afghanistan, commanders identified the need for a new initiative to counter new threats, emanating from the so-called Islamic State (IS) and other hostile actors. The invasion of Ukraine by Russia and the concern of the conflict spreading into western Europe added incentive to invest, form and deliver an operational capability that has readiness, punch, and flexibility to meet a wide-range of scenarios. As the British Army's rapid response formation, 16 AABCT is the largest brigade in the army, with 6,200 personnel. Spearheaded by two Parachute Regiment battalions it includes: one air assault infantry battalion, one light recce strike infantry battalion, one airborne close support artillery regiment, one close support air manoeuvre engineer regiment, an air assault logistics regiment, a manoeuvre medical regiment, a Communication and Information Support squadron, and a

Paratroopers, wearing the Low-Level-Parachute (LLP), board an Airbus A400M for a training jump. (MOD/Crown Copyright)

Prior to the GRF the Paras headed the Joint Rapid Response Force (JRRF). (Bob Jarvis/DPL)

Pathfinder platoon. Due to the brigade's mobile role, it is lightly armed and equipped. The brigade's land equipment includes Foxhounds, Jackals, WMIK Land Rovers, Supacat all-terrain vehicles, and 105mm light guns. The brigade's aviation support consists of three attack regiments equipped with Apache and Wildcat helicopters from the Army Air Corps as well as Chinook and Puma helicopters from the Joint Helicopter Command.

The Parachute Regiment's credentials as a fighting force made it the obvious selection as the lead component of the GRF. From the Middle East to Northern Ireland, the Falklands and Afghanistan, the Paras have been ➲

The force is equipped with light, highly mobile vehicles such as the Jackal seen here in Afghanistan.

The Land Rover WMIK currently remains in service with the heavy machine gun platoons. (DPL)

deployed on operations every year since they were formed – with the exception of 1968. Its hallmark of combat excellence has earned its premier status as the UK's shock troops. The regiment is the only unit within the regular army that still specially trains and selects its own officers and soldiers through a highly arduous selection process. It involves a series of tests designed to ensure that those who are successful have both the physical and mental fortitude to deploy on the most demanding type of operations anywhere in world at short notice.

A battalion equipped with the Low-Level-Parachute (LLP), can be dropped with equipment at 450ft from both port and starboard side doors from an Airbus A400M aircraft – in a procedure known as 'sim-sticks.' Parachuting as a method of entry offers a strategic delivery that was most recently used in Afghanistan in 2001 when elements of the

Heavy machine gun teams with WMIKS Land Rovers pictured during night firing. (MOD/Crown Copyright)

Communications teams from 216 Signals Squadron are integral to the regiment's capability. (DPL)

75th Ranger Regiment jumped into Kandahar to stage an assault on a target codenamed Objective Rhino. In 2003, the 173rd Airborne Regiment jumped into northern Iraq as part of Operation Iraqi Freedom and in 2018 the French 2nd REP dropped into the Méneka region of Mali in operations against IS fighters. The regiment's last airborne assault took place in 1956 when the 3rd Battalion dropped into El Gamil in Egypt alongside French forces following President Nasser's nationalisation of the Suez Canal. Since then, the Paras have been 'stood-up' for numerous airborne assaults and in 2006 when the 3rd Battalion planned two parachute assault operations in Afghanistan, both of which were postponed.

In 2023, after civil war erupted in Sudan the regiment was directed to plan a parachute assault to secure an airfield north of Khartoum prior to the evacuation of UK nationals. The aim was to remove rebel forces from the area - but the operation was cancelled, when it was established that there was no threat. The formation operates closely with the US Army's 82nd Airborne Division and this was demonstrated in 2021 when soldiers from 2nd Battalion the Parachute ➲

Training in areas such as Jordan, Oman, and Morocco are undertaken with partner forces. (MOD/Crown Copyright)

Parachuting regularly takes place with American and French partner forces. (MOD/Crown Copyright)

Paratroopers are trained to operate in the jungle environments of areas such as Belize and Brunei. (MOD/Crown Copyright)

Soldiers take part in routine training to ensure they are ready to deploy at short notice. (MOD/Crown Copyright)

Live firing exercises ensure paratroopers are at readiness to deploy. (16AABCT)

Regiment joined the 3rd Brigade Combat Team of the 82nd Airborne Division in a Joint Forcible Entry exercise, flying direct from the United States and parachuting into Estonia. Around 600 US and UK paratroopers made the 7,500km flight from Fort Bragg in North Carolina to Estonia jumping from USAF C-17 aircraft. In May 2023, UK paratroopers from 16 AABCT mounted a night jump alongside US, Czech Republic, Latvian, Polish, and Estonian allies as part of a large-scale American-led military exercise, called Exercise Swift Response.

Battalion Composition

The regiment has three regular battalions and one reserve battalion. The 1st Battalion is permanently under the command of the Director Special Forces and assigned to the role of the Special Forces Support Group (SFSG). It continues to draw its personnel from the Parachute Regiment. Both the ➲

The light 'man-portable' evolutionary NLAW anti-tank weapon is used by the Paras. (MOD/Crown Copyright)

Paratroopers pictured at 'action stations' inside an A400 just before they are called forward to jump. (MOD/Crown Copyright)

Soldiers exit from both doors of an A400 in a process called 'sim-sticks'. (MOD/Crown Copyright)

2nd and 3rd Battalions, as well as the 4th (Reserve) Battalion train as Air Manoeuvre Battle-Groups (AMBG) in a rotation of readiness. This is a combined arms force, which delivers broader capability calling on specialist artillery, engineer, communication, and medical skills from bespoke units with 16AABCT. Among these highly specialist units are 216 Parachute Signals Squadron, 7th Parachute Regiment Royal Horse Artillery, 23 Parachute Engineer Regiment, 13th Air Assault Regiment Royal Logistics Corps, and 16 Medical Regiment Royal Army Medical Corps. The brigade can also call on the Royal Gurkha Rifles and the Royal Irish Regiment who serve with the force in the important role of air assault infantry and would, if required deploy as 'air landed' troops or flown forward by helicopter in an air assault role.

Future tactics and procedures will ensure the that the 'high-readiness' battle-group will retain the parachute role while at the same time allowing the regiment to generate company 'strike' groups which can mount parachute operations alongside coalition forces. To develop this concept, company groups from ➲

Paras wait to board an A400M, their equipment packs which they jump with can been seen on the ground. (MOD/Crown Copyright)

Soldiers, wearing the LLP, line up and prepare to exit an A400M. (MOD/Crown Copyright)

A Tactical Air Landing Operation (TALO) can be mounted to reinforce capability at an air-head. (DPL)

The Hercules C130J, known as Fat Albert, was the work-horse of airborne operations for many years. (MOD/Crown Copyright)

Insertion can be mounted by Rapid Air Land (RAL) —in which the aircraft lands and troops exit at speed. (DPL)

Helicopter assault operations are a key part of modern-day airborne delivery. (Dil Banerjee/DPL)

both battalions have jumped with alliance partners across NATO using their canopies. The Parachute Regiment uses the LLP, which has now been in service for more than 20 years. It is a static line operated parachute assembly that allows fully equipped airborne troops to carry out massed tactical parachute assaults from jump heights as low as 76m (250ft). In training, paratroopers usually jump at 800ft with the safety ceiling set at 450ft for operational jumps. The LLP allows pilots to approach the drop zone (DZ) at low level, avoiding radar and air defence systems, then gain altitude to drop their paratroopers.

The canopy incorporates a number of proven features to meet operational requirements. These ensure fast and consistent openings, comfortable 'G' levels during canopy inflation, rapid damping of canopy oscillation, a low rate of descent and a high tolerance to prevent twisting of rigging lines. The arrival of the RAF's new Airbus A400M, known as the Atlas, has given a new focus to parachuting and successful trials took place on Salisbury Plain in late 2022. The jump programme was planned and delivered by No. 206 Squadron, the RAF's heavy aircraft

UK troops regularly jump with American forces parachuting from C-17 aircraft. (DPL)

UK and US paratroopers jump from a C-17, their equipment is still attached to their legs. (DPL)

Both 2 and 3 Parachute Battalions train for a wide range of tasks, such as riot control as pictured here in 2003.

transport aircraft to a Forward Operating Base (FOB) in Senegal in readiness to mount an evacuation in Sierra Leone. Insertion can also be mounted by Rapid Air Land (RAL) – a capability in which the aircraft lands, allows the troops to exit at speed from the rear ramp, and immediately lifts off again to avoid enemy attack. A second procedure is called a Tactical Air Landing Operation (TALO). A TALO can be mounted to reinforce capability at an air-head. This routinely requires an aircraft to land, unload its payload with engines running ready and quickly take-off – although not under the same time pressure as an RAL. The new Global Response Force, based around 16 AABCT, also includes the newly formed 1st Combat Aviation Brigade, equipped with Apache AH- 64E helicopters.

test and evaluation unit, who worked alongside the Joint Air Delivery Test and Evaluation Unit. RAF specialists from the Parachute Test Team assisted the paratroopers in dry training, fitting, and checking of equipment, prior to mounting the parachute trials.

Heliborne Assault

While the 'parachute role' remains the hallmark of the Parachute Regiment's methods of entry, the Paras also train to mount helicopter assaults – a role demonstrated in 1999 when the 1st Battalion was flown by helicopter air assault to a forming up position outside Kosovo, as part of a NATO operation. They then advanced into Pristina on foot. A year later in 2000, the battalion deployed by C-130J

Chinooks land on a bridge as they drop paratroopers on the outskirts of Kosovo in 1999.

The Army Air Corps' upgraded Apache helicopter will support 16 AABCT. (MOD/Crown Copyright)

The Pathfinders

The Pathfinder Platoon (PF) is the forward reconnaissance force of today's 16 Air Assault Brigade Combat Team and as such is on permanent readiness in support of the Air Manoeuvre Battle Group (AMBG). During deployments in Afghanistan the Pathfinders delivered significant 'surveillance and intelligence' contributions to support the commander's planning process. Prior to the arrival of the main force, they moved out into the open desert to evaluate the enemy's capability and dispositions. The PF was enhanced with a team of engineers from the brigade, as well as electronic warfare experts and a mechanic to maintain the vehicles. In a conventional conflict environment, the unit provides the advance force to facilitate theatre entry and subsequently form a mobile Long Range Reconnaissance Patrol (LRRP) working direct to the commander at 16 AABCT. Pathfinders usually operate in six- man teams. They can insert by air using High Altitude Low Opening (HALO) or High Altitude High Opening (HAHO) parachute skills across a range of parachute systems, including the BT80 multi-mission parachute combined with the High Altitude

Parachutist Life Support System, which provides oxygen when jumping at high altitude. On the ground, they identify the drop zone for a battalion and mark what is called the 'alpha' – the position on the ground for the lead aircraft to drop paratroopers – which at night is illuminated at the last minute. They then move forward to carry out surveillance of enemy forces and collate intelligence. The Pathfinder Platoon is around 60 men strong. Many of the volunteers come from the Parachute Regiment and across 16 AABCT, while entrance is accepted from across the armed forces. The group was formally established in 1985 having first been raised as far back as 1942, for wartime operations. In the aftermath of the Falklands conflict the brigade was re- established as an airborne force. Then a battalion drop required a formation of 15 Hercules aircraft to drop paratroopers and stores, over two drop zones in under five minutes, by day or night. To do this there was a requirement for the drop areas to be clearly marked, to ensure that the pilots and crews had an easily identified reference point to allow them to drop accurately and consistently. Pathfinders had established this role in World War Two. The demise of 16th Parachute Brigade in 1977 and the

disbandment of the Pathfinder Company (then managed by No 1 Guards Independent Company, The Parachute Regiment) meant that the expertise was lost. The capability was then reformed in 1985. From the beginning, much emphasis was placed on HALO as an insertion method. Pathfinder selection is open to soldiers of all cap badges. The selection cadre currently lasts six weeks and includes a rigorous process to test aptitude, endurance, and soldiering. Soldiers who successfully pass the cadre undergo a period of further in-depth weapons training, high altitude parachute training in America as well as Survival Escape Resistance and Evasion (SERE) training before joining the Pathfinders. The course consists of five aptitude phases, each of which has an element of training followed by assessment or test. Prior to phase one there are two entry tests that must be passed. The first is an eight-mile Combat Fitness Test over an unfamiliar route carrying 44lb, less food, water, and rifle. This must be completed in two hours. The second is a two-mile speed test which must be completed in 18 minutes or less. Volunteers must pass physical, navigation, demolition, and range tests as well as escape and evasion before a final exercise which incorporates all the skills.

Machine gun teams provide cover for advancing troops. (MOD/Crown Copyright)

Today GRF is the centrepiece of the UK's future readiness capability, ready to deploy at short notice in support of UK defence policy. The force is centred around an Air Manoeuvre Brigade Combat Team consisting of airborne, air assault and light infantry battalions, complemented by artillery, engineers, logistics, signals, intelligence as well as electronic and cyber-warfare specialists. This force can deploy small company strike groups or a battle-group of 650 paratroopers and support specialists and trains regularly for such eventualities. It was the Parachute Regiment who first deployed soldiers to provide security in Kabul in 2001 with 2 PARA arriving to commence security and stability duties as NATO's initial International Security and Assistance Force (ISAF) in Kabul. In the past two decades the tempo of operations for the Parachute Regiment has been 'high' with units deploying multiple times on operations, from Northern Ireland, to Macedonia, Kosovo, Sierra Leone, Afghanistan, and Iraq. ●

RAF Chinooks flew the 1st Battalion forward from Macedonia in 1999 – before they advance by foot into Pristina.

The Pathfinders are tasked to jump in ahead of the main assault force. (MOD/Crown Copyright)

A Pathfinder leaves the rear ramp of a C-130 during an insertion ahead of the main paratrooper force. (MOD/Crown Copyright)

On the ground, the Pathfinders use strategic communications equipment all over the globe. (Dil Banerjee/DPL)

Paras take part in helicopter operations with US troops in Macedonia. (MOD/Crown Copyright)

BRITAIN'S AIRB

Prime Minister Winston Churchill called for a force of 5,000
paratroopers to counter the German airborne shock troops. (ABF/DPL)

ORNE FORCES

Britain's airborne forces were raised after wartime Prime Minister Winston Churchill sought a counter to Hitler's 'shock troops' who had dropped ahead of the Nazi's conventional forces to seize objectives, with great success. As Britain faced its darkest hour Churchill, who had taken office on May 10, 1940, made his maiden speech to the House of Commons telling ministers that he had nothing to offer but 'blood, toil, tears and sweat'. Following the evacuation of Dunkirk, he warned the country about the risk of invasion, and he now looked to his military commanders to give him direction.

On June 22, 1940, Prime Minister Churchill, directed the War Office to investigate the possibility of forming a corps of at least 5,000 parachute-trained troops, which, he added, should include a proportion of Canadians, Australians, and New Zealanders. But the shortage of resources meant it was difficult to train any volunteers fully. Priority was given to the RAF, which desperately needed pilots and other aircrew trades to fight the Battle of Britain and develop the bomber force, while the army was still reorganising and re-arming at home and abroad. The prime minister told the Joint Chiefs of Staff: "We ought to have a corps of at least 5,000 parachute troops . . . advantage of the summer must be taken to train these troops, who can none the less play their part meanwhile as shock troops in home defence." Initially, 3,500 men volunteered for service, of whom 500 were further selected for parachute training. However, their training was held up owing to the lack of suitable aircraft. The American Douglas DC-3 Dakota was the preferred aircraft with its side exit door, but there were few available so it was decided that with minor modifications the British Armstrong Whitworth Whitley bomber could be adapted for parachuting, although these aircraft were also in limited supply. In addition, there were only a few civilian gliders, and these could not easily be converted for military operations owing to their light construction.

The twin-engine Whitley was considered suitable for parachuting because at the time

Today's paratroopers owe their heritage and history to those who pioneered the role back in the 1940s. (Dil Banerjee/DPL)

There was little room inside the bombers and in the early days soldiers wore a helmet with a rubber rim to protect their heads. (ABF/DPL)

Paratroopers drop from the bomb hole of a Whitley bomber. The opening was very small and left very little room for mistakes. (ABF/DPL)

it was the slowest of the available RAF aircraft and it also had the capability to tow gliders. However, these aircraft were primarily built for bombing and the long thin fuselage did not leave much room for paratroopers; the aircraft initially had capacity for just eight soldiers, later increasing to ten. The first jumps from the Whitleys were carried out on July 13, 1940, by RAF Parachute Jump Instructors and men from No 2 Commando. It was this unit that would form the 1st Parachute Battalion in September 1941. One at a time, a parachutist and a dispatcher crawled on their hands and knees to the rear of the aircraft, where the gun turret had been removed.

There they knelt in the open tail of the Whitley ready to make their jump. Holding on to a small metal bar, the jumper positioned himself carefully on a small platform, about one foot square, and then stood up. Standing outside the aircraft and exposed to the elements, the jumper went through the drill with the instructor; then, when he was given the signal, he pulled his ripcord. Within seconds the slipstream caught hold of the parachute and

Volunteers who signed up for Churchill's new airborne forces jumped with no reserve chute. (DPL)

Static lines can be seen in the doorway and the top of the parachute is fixed by a small tie called an 'apex'; these are still used to pull open the canopy as they were in the 1940s. (Fin Reynolds/DPL)

An early paratrooper drops through the bomb hole of a Whitley bomber. (War Office/DPL Archives)

number one launched himself through the hole while trying to maintain the position of attention. This was important in order to get the exit just right. Too hard a push-off could result in the jumper smashing his face against the opposite side of the hole, while too feeble an effort caused the parachute pack on the man's back to catch on the edge of the hole and tip him forward, with the same outcome. Hitting the side of the hole during an exit was known as 'ringing the bell'.

The first jump by a pupil at Ringway took place from a Whitley on July 21, 1940. Just four days later, on July 25, Private Evans, a driver with the Royal Army Service Corps who had volunteered for special service, was killed when his parachute rigging lines twisted around his canopy, preventing it from deploying. His jump was only the 136th since Ringway had opened and training was suspended for several weeks while trials with dummies were carried out. It was at this point that Raymond Quilter of the GQ Parachute Company demonstrated a new parachute system which he had designed with his colleague James Gregory. The system used ➲

opened it, jerking the jumper away from the aircraft. It was a crude and risky procedure, but the shortage of aircraft had forced the staff to improvise and adapt the Whitley in the best way they could, with the only parachute available to them.

Shortly after training commenced the instructors decided to tie a secure line to the ripcord which was then fastened in the aircraft with the aim of achieving automatic opening. This system worked well at first, but it was very dangerous, and a number of parachutists lost their lives. The system meant that now parachuting would be from an exit inside the aircraft, not from side doors like American paratroopers in their Dakotas, but from a hole in the floor of the Whitley bomber. This exit needed maximum courage, although it was perhaps an improvement on standing in the open air at the back of the rear turret. On the order 'Action Stations', the first two jumpers sat opposite each other with their feet dangling out through the hole. On the order 'Go' the

A soldier holds himself perfectly straight as drops through the bomb hole of a Whitley bomber. (War Office/DPL Archives)

Prime Minister Sir Winston Churchill visited Ringway to see progress for himself. (War Office/DPL Archives)

Paratroopers who have just jumped put on a display for Mr Churchill. (War Office/DPL Archives)

and GQ, who continue to supply parachutes to Britain's airborne forces today. Jumping resumed two weeks after the death of Private Evans using the new static line parachute. But despite the improved mechanics the difficulty in making a good clean exit from the 'hole' in the Whitley often resulted in 'twists' and more accidents. These horrific incidents, in which twisted rigging lines prevented the parachutes from deploying, became known as 'Roman Candles' and were greatly feared by trainees. In the first few months of operations at Ringway more than 2,000 descents had been recorded but by the end of 1940 at least three men had died. The 'Roman Candle' was - and still is - the greatest fear of any paratrooper.

In September 1940 the school at Ringway was expanded to become the Central Landing Establishment and was divided into a Parachute Training School, a Technical Unit, and a Glider Training Squadron. The role of the establishment was to train parachute troops, glider pilots, and aircrew for airborne work, develop the tactical handling of airborne

The need for parachute packers was now vital and the women in the RAF prepared thousands of canopies. (War Office/DPL Archives)

Physical fitness was paramount, and volunteers were tested before being accepted onto a jumps course. (War Office/DPL Archives)

the same 28ft canopy, packed in a bag carried on the soldier's back. A static line was fitted to the apex, the top of the parachute, and secured inside the aircraft. This enabled the rigging lines to be pulled out and fully extended before the canopy deployed. It also had the advantage of delaying opening until the parachute was well clear of the aircraft. The parachute itself broke away from the soldier's back and remained attached to the static line and the aircraft. As he continued to fall, his weight pulled first the lift webs, then the rigging lines, out of the bag. Finally, at the end of the taut and extended rigging lines, the canopy pulled out of the bag, a final tie broke, and the canopy developed. The opening shock was negligible and the danger of becoming entangled was also greatly reduced. Within five days of the first fatality, a modified version of the GQ system was being developed in conjunction with Irvin Parachutes to produce the GQ X-Type static chute system. This very effective system remained in service for the remainder of the World War Two. It was produced by two rival companies, Irvin,

Soldiers check each other's parachutes at Ringway before being sent to their respective battalions. (War Office/DPL Archives)

The static lines can be seen as these soldiers exit the aircraft, they will pull taut and pull open the canopy. (War Office/DPL Archives)

A colleague helps a fellow Para fix the leg straps to the d-ring in the centre of the chest. (War Office/DPL Archives)

Exiting the aircraft, this paratrooper can be seen with his equipment valise which carries his back back and other items. (War Office/DPL Archives)

troops, carry out technical research, and recommend operational requirements. In the same month, in a report to the prime minister, the Air Ministry proposed the following tasks for which airborne troops could be used: a parachute raid on a selected position followed by evacuation by air; a parachute raid followed by evacuation by sea; dropping parachutists secretly to act as saboteurs. The ministry concluded that for any operation about 1,000 men would be needed of whom just 100 would parachute in, while 900 would be glider-borne. The report recommended that the total airborne force should comprise 500 parachute troops, 2,700 glider troops and 360 glider pilots to fly the glider-borne troops. The number of parachutists was considerably lower than initially planned. At the end of 1940 the Air Ministry and War Office had agreed to produce four types of glider. The four were an eight-seater to be named the Hotspur, a 25-seater named the Horsa, a 15-seater to be produced in small numbers and called the Hengist, and a large glider called the Hamilcar which could carry either a tank or 40 troops.

By early 1941 the first 500 parachutists had been trained for operations and in April that year the first service gliders, Hotspurs, arrived at Ringway. On April 26, 1941, a parachute and glider demonstration was held at Ringway for Prime Minister Churchill. A formation of six

Whitleys dropped just 60 men - considerably fewer than the prime minister had expected to see, but as many as could take part owing to the small number of suitable aircraft available. Due to this

lack of available aircraft, the Air Ministry wanted to cut the target number of parachute troops from 5,000 to 500 and was in the process of presenting papers to justify their arrival at this reduced ➲

Paratroopers assist each other with the harness of their canopies. Once on the ground they removed themselves from the parachute by turning the release ring, seen in the centre of their chests. (War Office/DPL Archives)

Whitley bombers dropped the Paras into France on Operation Biting; the soldiers can be seen exiting underneath the planes. (War Office/DPL Archives)

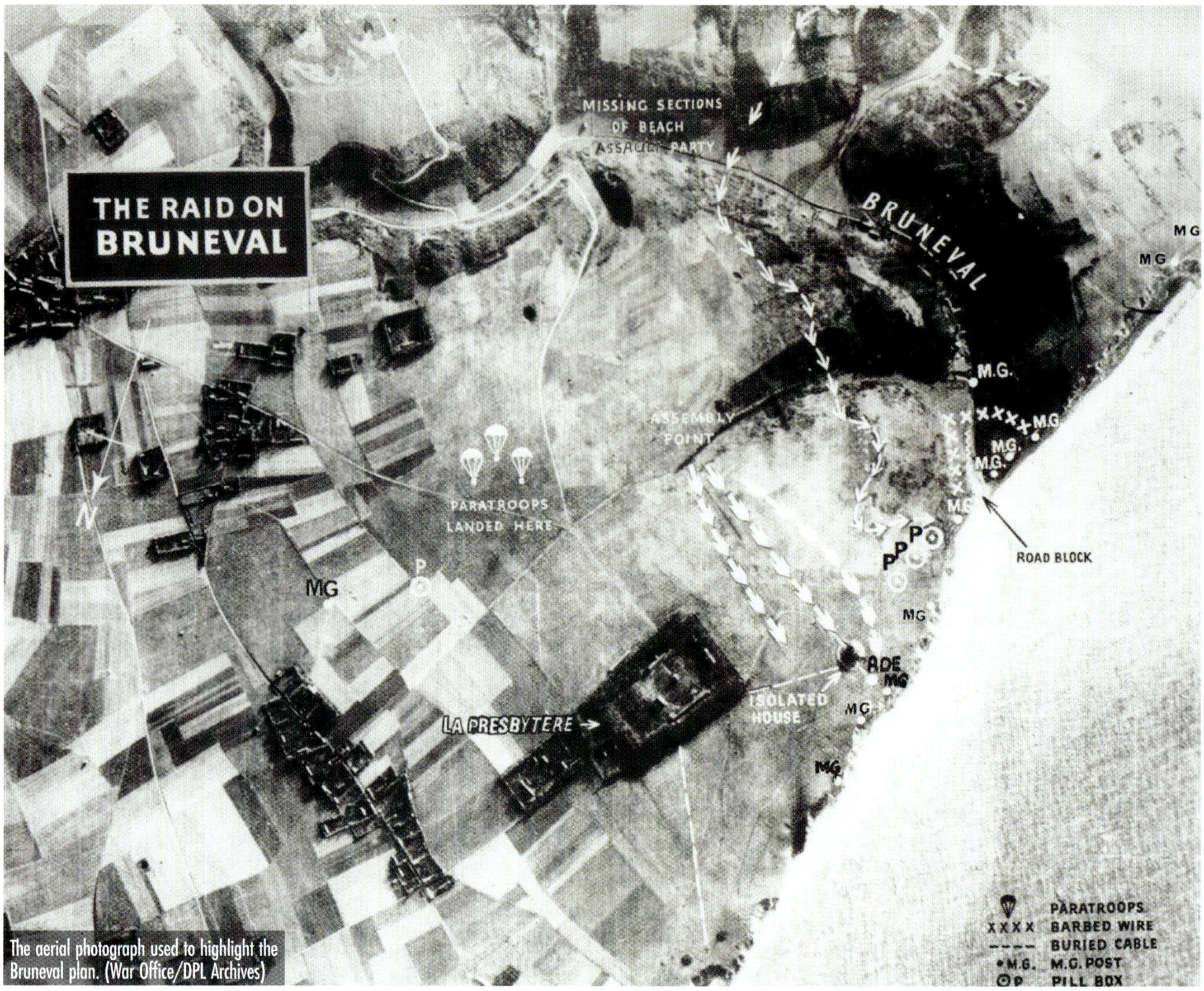

The aerial photograph used to highlight the Bruneval plan. (War Office/DPL Archives)

Soldiers had undergone parachute training at Ringway and were now ready to drop into France. (War Office/DPL Archives)

bomber was the only aircraft the RAF approved for jumping. The only para-trained troops were the 11th Special Air Service, formed from No 2 Commando in November 1940. Codenamed Operation Colossus the mission involved jumping into Italy and blowing up an aqueduct. Water from the Tragino aqueduct was pumped by pipeline to supply Italian forces and was the perfect target to gain maximum propaganda, destroying the enemy's morale. But it was too far inland for a seaborne raid and too difficult

figure. However, at the same time, the prime minister wanted an update on the progress of his 'direction' for a force of 5,000 and before the RAF could present their justification, the German 7th Airborne Division mounted a successful airborne assault on Crete. It was an operation the RAF had previously advised was not possible and the deciding factor for Churchill that airborne troops were needed. He asked his chiefs of staff for proposals to ensure that the original target figure of 5,000 was met as soon as possible.

Operations Colossus and Biting

Britain's first airborne operation took place in early 1941 while the fledgling force was still developing and even before the Ringway demonstrations. There were few dedicated resources to support parachuting and the Whitley

John Frost , the company commander who led the operation into France, can be seen on the right. (War Office/DPL Archives)

Rehearsals took place in preparation for Operation Biting, many of the soldiers has still not been issued with their red berets. (War Office/DPL Archives)

Numerous drills took place to make sure the paratroopers were familiar with the Operation Biting plan and the naval landing craft. (War Office/DPL Archives)

to bomb. An airborne assault was the obvious answer, and it was the opportunity Whitehall Chiefs had been seeking to test Churchill's new force, which was only seven months old.

In total, 38 men of what was then called the 11th Special Air Service Battalion dropped from two Whitley bombers, having had just three weeks of training, in which one man, L/ Sgt Dennis, was killed when he landed in a lake and drowned. The raid took place on the night of February 10, 1941, and it was intended that after blowing up the aqueduct, the unit would make their way to the coast to be picked up by the submarine HMS *Triumph*. The objective was destroyed, but the entire force was captured as they headed for the rendezvous with the

senior service. It later transpired that one of the Whitley planes which had dropped the men, had crashed near the spot where the *Triumph* was due to surface and had been diverted away after enemy warships searched for the plane's aircrew.

It was almost a year later that the regiment was called on to carry out a daring 'behind the lines' raid, of vital importance to the war office. The operation was so successful that it attracted applause from Prime Minister Winston Churchill and guaranteed the Paras' wartime future. The aim of Operation Biting was to dismantle a Wurzburg precision radar dish - one of a series of early warning installations on the north coast of France - and bring it back to England for scientific research. Admiral Lord Mountbatten had proposed the raid, after it became clear that this established chain of radar stations was of significant importance to the ➲

The plan was to parachute in, recover the radar and then exit by sea, thanks to the Royal Navy. (War Office/DPL Archives)

Frost and his men return from a successful Operation Biting. (War Office/DPL Archives)

Paratroopers return from Operation Biting on a Royal Navy launch. (War Office/DPL Archives)

Luftwaffe, who were inflicting heavy losses on RAF Bomber Command. But the radar posts were heavily defended against attack from the sea with machine guns looking down onto the beach and hidden barbed wire surrounding the radars. It was a task only airborne troops could accomplish. When the RAF brought back pictures of a radar system near Le Havre, situated high on an isolated clifftop near the village of Bruneval, the Chief of Combined Operations agreed to mount a recovery raid aimed at bringing elements of the dish back to the UK for research. The task was given to Major John Frost and his men of C Company (Charlie) 2nd Parachute Battalion, otherwise known within the brigade as 'Jock' company, for its obvious high contingent of troops from Scottish regiments. They were to be dropped into France in three separate groups and carry out their mission with the support of an RAF radar expert and then be picked up by a mini flotilla of six Royal Navy landing craft. In recognition of the joint operation with the Admiralty, each group of 40 Paras was named after a famous sailor, 'Nelson', 'Drake', and 'Rodney' - a gesture to the senior service which was never forgotten by the navy. On the night of February 27, 1942, the 120-strong force took off from Thruxton Aerodrome in a fleet

Glider development was now in full production, although there was little room inside for soldiers. (War Office/DPL Archives)

The US-built Dakota would eventually enter service and allow British paratroopers to jump from a side door. (MOD/Crown Copyright)

of 12 Whitley bombers, each carrying 10 men, and jumped in perfect weather conditions into France.

The operation met strong resistance, three men were killed and a further seven badly injured. But it had been a success, the vital equipment secured, and a German radar expert captured. Of these first airborne operations perhaps the least known is Operation Fresh-man, which involved glider borne troops of the Royal Engineers in November 1942. In this, the first glider assault, airborne troops were tasked to land in northern Norway and destroy the Norsk Hydro plant.

Red Devils

The famous red beret was first seen by German troops in North Africa and within months they had christened the ferocious Paras 'Rote Teufel' - Red Devils. This distinctive head dress, since adopted by parachute troops all over the world, was officially introduced in 1942, at the direction of General Browning, and along with the Pegasus symbol - Bellerophon astride winged Pegasus - became the emblem of British airborne forces. Allied forces had invaded Algeria and Morocco on November 8, in an operation which was planned to cut off German supply routes from Europe. Days later the 3rd Battalion made the first operational battalion drop in a successful assault at Bone airfield, on November 12.

The 1st Parachute Brigade, comprising three battalions and supporting elements, were sent to north Africa by sea - except the 3rd Battalion, who had been airlifted for the Bone assault from St Eval in Cornwall, travelling via Gibraltar. Later, when the Paras captured a group of 200 Germans in February 1943, they discovered the Nazis were carrying special instructions, telling how best to fight the Rote Teufel (the Red Devils). The Paras were overjoyed at the respect they had gained from the Germans. General Haig congratulated them, and General Browning sent a message saying 'Such distinctions are seldom given in war and then only to the finest fighting troops'.

In November 1942, Lieutenant Colonel John Frost, who was now commanding the 2nd Battalion was tasked to mount an operation against enemy held airfields

The Parachute Regiment now found itself deployed to North Africa where the Germans dubbed them 'Red Devils' (War Office/DPL Archives)

The Paras were now in North Africa fighting Rommel's Nazis. (War Office/DPL Archives)

The regiment fought in Greece and Sicily before preparing for the invasion of Europe. (War Office/DPL Archives)

near Depienne, 30 miles south of Tunis. The battalion dropped, but found the airfield was abandoned and a column of armour scheduled to meet up with the 2nd Battalion at Oudna never arrived, leaving them abandoned 50 miles behind enemy lines. They were soon attacked and heavily outnumbered by German units but fought like lions to battle their way back to Allied lines in a series of ambushes and fire fights, which left 16 officers and 250 men killed and wounded.

In June 1943, the 2nd and 4th Parachute Brigades as well as the 1st Air Landing Brigade, had joined the depleted 1st Brigade in north Africa to form the 1st Airborne Division, as preparations were made for further operations, into Italy and Sicily. On July 13, more than 112 aircraft and 16 gliders carrying 1,856 men, took off from north Africa. Their initial target was to capture the Primosole bridge and the high ground around it, providing a pathway for the 8th Army, but heavy anti-aircraft fire shot down many of the Dakotas before sticks could even jump out. Only 295 officers and men were dropped close enough to carry out the assault on the bridge. ●

P Company is the selection course that soldiers must pass before they can start parachute training. (DPL)

THE SELECTION PROCESS
P COMPANY

Legendary across the British Army, **P Company** is the selection course that soldiers must pass before they can start parachute training. Potential recruits to the Parachute Regiment and volunteers from support arms who wish to serve with airborne forces must pass this evaluation. It is a raw assessment of physical ability and mental resilience that pushes men and women to their breaking point in a series of tests that demand focus and the requirement to demonstrate confidence at height as well as the ability to fight an opponent in hand-to-hand combat. It is this training that shapes the modern paratrooper as a confident, balanced soldier ready to deploy on a scenario of operations.

Recruits to the Parachute Regiment undergo Phase One and Two infantry training at Catterick and are then loaded onto Pre-Parachute Selection – otherwise known as P Company. This progression qualifies a soldier to go forward and undertake parachute training. After several weeks of preparation candidates face a series of eight tests which test an individuals' courage and determination to succeed. This process has been retained since the Parachute Regiment was first formed. Those who volunteer must demonstrate they have the confidence to operate at height and deliver the personal resilience to never give up in the face of adversity. From the pioneering days at Ringway to today's course at Catterick the physical standard remains the same, as does the justification for such high standards. Within minutes of arriving on the drop zone paratroopers must be ready to move away from the area at speed in order avoid enemy indirect fire, such as mortar and artillery bombardments, which is highly likely to reign down as soon as the airborne force is identified. To counter this, soldiers must get out of their parachute-harness, reach their assembly points, and leave the area ➲

Recruits to the Parachute Regiment undergo Phase One and Two infantry training at Catterick and are then loaded onto Pre-Parachute Selection. (MOD/Crown Copyright)

After several weeks of preparation candidates face a series of eight trials which test an individuals' courage and determination to succeed. (MOD/Crown Copyright)

All Bergen rucksacks are weighed to ensure recruits are carrying the same amount. (MOD/Crown Copyright)

Recruits are not allowed a sling on their weapon. These rookies are pictured in Brecon in the mid-1990s. (Dil Banerjee/DPL)

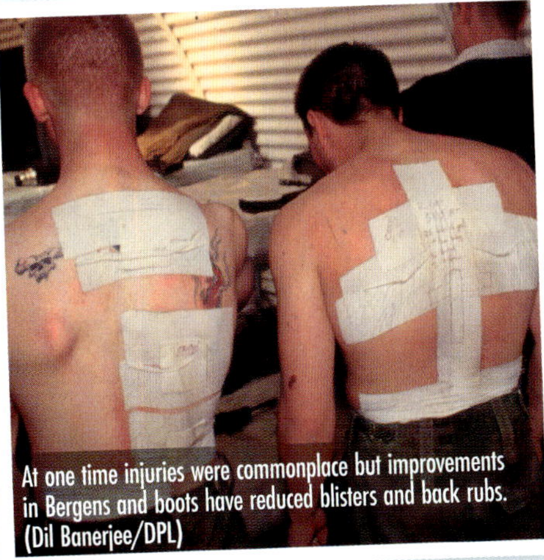

At one time injuries were commonplace but improvements in Bergens and boots have reduced blisters and back rubs. (Dil Banerjee/DPL)

At the end of a run recruits will be tested further by spending some time running up and down a hill to see who survives. (Dil Banerjee/DPL)

Speed marches are a key part of the P Company regime. (Fin Reynolds/DPL)

as quickly as possible – a tactic developed during World War Two and remains just as important today. The early days of physical training prior to parachute training was seen as critical to avoid soldiers constantly getting injured when jumping. An initial Airborne Forces Depot was formed at Hardwick Hall in 1942 and oversaw the training of recruits, before they went to the Parachute Training School at Ringway. Then, in 1946 instruction moved to Albany Barracks on the Isle of Wight before transferring to Maida Barracks in Aldershot, where it remained for 22 years before moving to Browning Barracks in Aldershot in 1968. As part of the military's re-organisation in the 1990s the selection process moved to Catterick in Yorkshire, where it remains.

Rookies who arrive at Catterick face an austere regime which seeks to test recruits from the day they arrive. Each candidate is given a number, which is worn on their helmet and smock. Instructors refer to each recruit as 'Joe' rather than use their name, an added factor to unsettle volunteers. In fact, it is another tradition of the regiment. The first volunteers for Para training in 1942 had their documents stamped with the letters JOE, standing for 'Joined on Enlistment'.

The course is designed around speed to reinforce the regiment's combat requirement to leave the drop zone as quickly as they can. Due to the 'light role' of the Parachute Regiment ➲

P Company have used South Wales, but most of the events are held in the hills around Catterick in Yorkshire. (Dil Banerjee/DPL)

The assault course may appear easy, but it is raced against the clock. (MOD/Crown Copyright)

Officers wear white shirts and enlisted soldiers' red on the course so that instructors can identify them easily. (DPL)

The stretcher race involves six soldiers carrying a metal frame, anyone caught falling back risks a chalk mark on their helmet and the possibility of being failed. (MOD/Crown Copyright)

and 16 Air Assault Brigade Combat Team (16AABCT) soldiers need to be able to march long distances with all their equipment and be ready to fight when they reach their objective - as demonstrated by the success of the 2nd and 3rd Battalions when they marched across the Falklands in 1982. In Parachute Regiment parlance covering such distance is known as a 'tactical advance to battle' or TAB.

The initial days of P Company are spent in the gym, racing around the camp and physically conditioning soldiers for the 'hills and the tests' ahead. There is little rest and

The Trainasium is a confidence test and requires a recruit to stand at the top and shout out his or her name, rank, and number. (Dil Banerjee/DPL)

Para Clothing

Today, boots and clothing are of a high standard unlike the basic items worn by rookies who underwent training back in World War Two. They initially wore heavy ammunition boots and serge trousers, which were far from comfortable for those undergoing parachute selection. Several innovative boots were developed in the 1940s, but the basic boot, made by John White Ltd, remained the main footwear of wartime Paras. By 1944 the first phase of specialist clothing was introduced with the most notable being the Denison smock .

Major Denison designed this baggy smock to be worn over the wartime battledress and became the iconic jacket of British airborne forces. It is still in service today, in an upgraded design and produced in modern day camouflage. The baggy design allows soldiers to jump during training exercises with a large parachute bag packed inside their smock, which once on the ground they can use to pack away the parachute for re-use. On operations they can also wear body armour under the smock.

recruits work long days often surviving on adrenaline. Enlisted personnel wear maroon t-shirts, while officers wear white t-shirts – allowing the instructors to identify them easily. Officers are expected to perform better than the soldiers they will lead and any officer who falls behind risks being taken off the course. Instructors are drawn from the Parachute Regiment, the Army Physical Training Corps, and the support arms cap badges who support 16 AABCT. They wear blue tracksuit ➲

Rookies are given their scores at the end of an event.

Jumping the net on the confidence course. (Will Taylor/DPL)

The milling is a test of personal confidence. (MOD/Crown Copyright)

of the tests is an event simply called 'milling'. This is a face-to-face test of controlled aggression in which soldiers wear a helmet guard and 16 oz gloves and fight for one minute. They must not shy away or turn their back on their opponent – if they do, they face being called back into the ring for a second time.

The day starts early on P Company with breakfast at 5.30am and a room inspection before forming up outside their block ready for the day's training. The night before, those on the course will need to make sure that their clothing is washed and ironed, boots immaculate and their Bergen (backpack) and fighting order is ready to go. Water bottles should be full all the time and equipment must be to the exact 35lb weight required. Anyone who fails to attend with the correct weight will have rocks added to their kit and those who arrive with water bottles that are not full can expect to have the contents poured over them. Instructors tell volunteers to believe in themselves and not question their own competence – but some will fall by the wayside. Each run or physical event is attended by medics and safety vehicles and instructors are trained to spot the signs of heat exhaustion and extreme fatigue, which will often result in staff telling rookies to get in the safety truck. During Test Week, candidates will be expected

Instructors oversee the milling – each recruit is marked, and a winner announced. (MOD/Crown Copyright)

Recruits at the top of Pen-y-fan in the mid-1990s. (Dil Banerjee/DPL)

jackets to identify themselves as P Company instructors and are called 'staff' by rookies.

The course is shaped around preparing soldiers for the challenges of airborne operations through a series of timed tests and evaluations. The selection includes a ten-mile march with full equipment, and an aerial confidence course 60ft above the ground called the Trainasium - which is designed to test a soldier's belief in him or herself. A log race in which the recruits carry the log for 1.9 miles tests determination; while the distance may sound easier - the speed is challenging. The 20-mile endurance march is a test of stamina and endurance, again against the clock. Finally, the Stretcher race, often called the 'sickener', involves a 16 strong team carrying a heavy metal stretcher over five miles – no more than four soldiers can carry the stretcher at any time as instructors swap them around. The Steeplechase includes a timed run, followed by the assault course over a 1.8-mile circuit. Of the seven 'scored' events a maximum of ten points can be awarded for each.

The course delivers the confidence to stand in the doorway and jump into the open sky at night, carrying Bergen and rifle. Among the most feared

Soldiers near finish line on the stretcher race. (MOD/Crown Copyright)

to run, march, and carry dead weights over distances up to 20 miles on undulating terrain.

A candidate who fails to display the appropriate level of self discipline and motivation throughout test week will fail the course. The test phase starts on a Wednesday morning and will finish the following Tuesday. The Trainasium is a simple pass or fail and ⮑

Eight soldiers man the log and must keep their hands ahead of the rope – those who fall off will be put in the safety vehicle. (MOD/Crown Copyright)

The log race is fast and furious. (DPL)

An instructor gives a recruit some gentle encouragement. (MOD/Crown Copyright)

A soldier ploughs through the water dip on the assault course. (David Reynolds)

Recruits race towards the finish line on the log race. (MOD/Crown Copyright)

Having passed P Company, successful candidates start the RAF basic parachute course at Brize Norton. (MOD/Crown Copyright)

Soldiers face several weeks of ground training to make sure they know how to land properly and pack their equipment. (MOD/Crown Copyright)

The P Company course sergeant major gives recruits their scores at the end of test week. (MOD/Crown Copyright)

Once trained, the trainees will make the first of eight training jumps. (MOD/Crown Copyright)

King Charles III, underwent parachute training when the was the Prince of Wales. (MOD/Crown Copyright)

involves the so called 'shuffle bars' which for many are mentally challenging and the hardest part of the obstacle. Here recruits are required to 'shuffle' along two scaffolding poles at the top of a 60ft tower, then with arms spread, shout out their name, rank, and number. The event is not hard, but it is a test of confidence as the brain is constantly saying this is not normal. As the week gets underway instructors will monitor recruits constantly, seeking to identify people who are not giving 100%. Recruits who do not deliver will get a chalk mark applied to the back of their helmet by an instructor – too many chalk marks will result in the rookie being pulled off the event. On the log race, those who fall behind the knot of their rope handle attached to the log can expect to get a white chalk mark on the back of their helmet. Weather, unless extreme, is rarely an obstacle, and events will take place in rain , wind, and snow.

In February 2020, Captain Rosie Wild, 28, of the Royal Artillery, became the first female officer to pass the All-Arms Pre-Parachute Selection course, more commonly known as P Company. Then in October 2022 Private Addy Carter, a medic with 16 Medical Regiment became the first female soldier to pass P Company. Pte Carter said : "Physically I found it very challenging, but it's about showing that you can deliver when things get hard - I just kept telling myself that every step was a step closer to the end". ●

THE AMERICAN AIRBORNE

Soldiers of the 82nd Airborne Division in a firefight in Afghanistan. (US DoD)

British airborne forces have continued to maintain close links with their **US airborne** counterparts since they fought alongside each other in World War Two. In particular, 16 Air Assault Brigade Combat Team (16 AABCT) is closely associated with the 82nd Airborne Division (82nd AB) and maintains an officer exchange programme with the unit. In 1996 the two forces deployed on Exercise Purple Star in which the entire UK force joined the 82nd AB in the biggest night parachute drop since 1944. This close bond and operational readiness has matured and today UK paratroopers are trained to operate with the US Global Response Force. The joint force has regularly demonstrated its strategic capability with UK and US paras flying more than 6,000 miles from the United States to parachute into Europe.

The 82nd Airborne Division, known as 'America's Guard of Honor', serve in a division with a proud history and well-deserved reputation. Originally formed as the 82nd Infantry Division on August 25, 1917, at Camp Gordon, Georgia, the 82nd soldiers were nicknamed the 'All-Americans' when it was discovered that the division contained men from every state in the union. The nickname resulted in the famous 'AA' shoulder patch, which 82nd paratroopers still wear proudly today. The division deployed to France in the spring of 1918 and in nearly five months of combat, the 82nd fought in three major campaigns and helped break the fighting spirit of the Kaiser's army. Two wartime 82nd soldiers earned the Medal of Honor, America's highest decoration for valour.

Lieutenant Colonel Emory J. Pike, division machine-gun officer, was conducting a frontline reconnaissance mission on September 15, 1918, near Vandieras, France, when heavy artillery shelling disrupted the advance of his division units. Pike reorganised the units and secured ➲

The 'All American' shoulder insignia of the 82nd Airborne Division. (US DoD)

A soldier of the 82nd Airborne returning fire with a machine gun in Afghanistan. (US DoD)

The 82nd Airborne jumping with the T10 canopy. (US DoD)

Soldiers from the 82nd Airborne descend using the new T-11 canopy which is bigger than the T10 and allows troops to jump with more equipment. (DPL)

A British paratrooper from 3rd Battalion Parachute Regiment prepares to jump with the 82nd AB. (US DoD)

US soldiers of the 82nd AB carrying electronic warfare equipment. (US DoD)

A sharpshooter with the 82nd AB in Afghanistan. (US DoD)

the position against enemy attack. He was severely wounded by shell fire when he went to the aid of a wounded soldier at an outpost.

Corporal Alvin C. York, Company 'G', 328th Infantry, earned his Medal of Honour for bravery in action near Chatel-Chéhery, France, on October 8, 1918. York took command of his platoon after three non-commissioned officers had been wounded or killed. He fearlessly charged a machine-gun nest, capturing four German officers, 128 men, and several weapons.

The 82nd was demobilised after World War One and for more than 20 years, the 'All-Americans' would live only in the memories of men who served in its ranks during the conflict. However, with the outbreak of the World War Two, the 82nd was reactivated on March 25, 1942, at Camp Claiborne, Louisiana, under the command of Major General Omar Bradley. On August 15 of that year, the 82nd became the first airborne division in the US Army, redesignated as the 82nd Airborne Division. In August 1942, the 82nd set sail for North Africa to fight the Third Reich. The division's first two combat operations were parachute and glider assaults into Sicily and Salerno, Italy, on July 9, and September 13, 1943.

While temporarily detached from the division, the 504th Parachute Infantry Regiment earned the nickname 'Devils

Originally formed as the 82nd Infantry Division on August 25, 1917, the unit served in France, October 1918. (US DoD)

Members of the 508th PIR, 82nd Airborne Division, check their equipment before taking off from an airfield in Saltby in Leicestershire to participate in the invasion of Europe, 1944. (US DoD)

The 82nd AB was sent into Panama in 1989 tasked with ousting a ruthless dictator and restoring the duly elected government to power. (US DoD)

in Baggy Pants' for their fighting prowess in the conflict at Anzio in January 1944. The remainder of the division had, meanwhile, pulled out of Italy in the autumn and moved on to England to prepare for the liberation of Europe. With two combat jumps under its belt, the division was ready for the most ambitious operation of the war, the invasion of Europe. On June 6, 1944, the 82nd's paratroopers and glider-borne soldiers boarded hundreds of aircraft bound for France.

By the time the 82nd was pulled back to England following D-Day, it had seen 33 days of intense combat and had reported 5,245 paratroopers killed, wounded, or missing. The Division's post-battle report read … '33 days of action without relief, without replacements. Every mission accomplished. No ground gained was ever relinquished.' Following the Normandy invasion, the 82nd became part of the newly organised XVIII Airborne Corps, which consisted of the US Army's 17th, 82nd and 101st Airborne Divisions. In 1944, the 82nd began preparing for Operation Market Garden in Holland. On September 17, the 82nd Airborne Division conducted its fourth combat jump of the war into Holland. Fighting off ferocious German counterattacks and was then ordered back to France.

On December 16, 1944, the Germans launched a surprise offensive through the Ardennes Forest which caught the Allies completely off guard. Two days later the 82nd joined in the fighting and General George Patton was so impressed with the 82nd's honour guard that he said: "In all my years in the army and all the honour guards I have ever seen, the 82nd's honour guard is undoubtedly the best." Hence the 'All Americans' became known as 'America's Guard of Honour'.

Post-War Years

In the post-war years, the 82nd made its permanent base at Fort Bragg, North Carolina, and was designated a regular army division

Units of the 82nd constantly train in readiness to be deployed anywhere across the globe. (US DoD)

Parachuting is the core form of insertion for the 82nd AB and night training jumps are regularly conducted. (US DoD)

A Chinook lifts off from a remote base of the 82nd Airborne during Operation Desert Storm in 1991. (US DoD)

in 1948. Life in the 82nd during the 1950s and '60s consisted of intensive training exercises in all environments and locations, including Alaska, Panama, the Far East, and the continental United States. The 82nd Airborne Division was again called to action during the Tet Offensive, which swept across the Republic of Vietnam in January 1968, the 3rd Brigade was alerted and within 24 hours was en route to Chu Lai. The 3rd Brigade performed combat ➲

The division trains to operate in all weathers from the jungle and desert as well as mountain and Arctic warfare. (US DoD)

Paratroopers from the 1st Combat Team firing anti-tank missiles during pre-deployment training. (US DoD)

When on standby potential deployment paratroopers undergo a 'combat readiness' package of training. (US DoD)

duties in the Hue-Phu-Bai area of the sector. Later, the brigade was moved south to Saigon, and fought battles in the Mekong Delta, the Iron Triangle, and along the Cambodian border. After serving nearly 22 months in Vietnam, the 3rd Brigade troopers returned to Fort Bragg in December 1969. During the 1970s division units were deployed to the Republic of Korea, Turkey, and Greece for exercises in potential battlegrounds often training with UK paratroopers. Then, in May 1978, the division was alerted for a possible drop into Zaire; again, in November 1979, the division was made ready for a possible operation to rescue American hostages in Iran, both were cancelled.

The 82nd AB deployed on operations in Grenada and later into Honduras as part of Operation Golden Pheasant. The deployment was billed as a joint training exercise, but the paratroopers were ready to fight. The introduction of armed paratroopers into the

Until the mid-2000s soldiers jumped with the oval shaped T10 canopy, as seen in this picture. It is being replaced with a larger T11 parachute. (US DoD)

A small number of Recon units of the 82nd are trained in HALO and work with US Special Forces. (US DoD)

Advanced communications are a fundamental requirement for today's airborne forces. (US DoD)

Soldiers of the 82nd AB exit a C-17 aircraft at first light. (US DoD)

Honduran countryside caused the Sandinistas to withdraw back to Nicaragua. On December 20, 1989, America's Guard of Honour, as part of Operation Just Cause, conducted their first combat jump since World War Two on to Torrijos International Airport, Panama. The paratroopers' goal was to oust a ruthless dictator and restore the duly elected government to power.

Seven months later they were in the Middle East, after the Iraqi invasion of Kuwait in August 1990. The 82nd became the vanguard of the largest movement of American troops since Vietnam. On January 16, 1991, Operation Desert Storm began when an armada of coalition war planes pounded Iraqi targets. The ground war got under way almost six weeks later. On February 23, the vehicle-mounted 82nd Airborne Division paratroopers protected the XVIII Airborne Corps' flank as fast-moving armoured and mechanised units moved deep inside Iraq.

Soldiers train to avoid hitting each other in the air which can result in what is called an 'air steal' in which one canopy consumes the air of another parachutist. (US DoD)

The 82nd operates the M-119 howitzer which can be airlifted into combat. (US DoD)

After the liberation of Kuwait, the 82nd began its redeployment back to Fort Bragg. Fort Bragg has more than 75 modern, well-maintained firing ranges and impact areas, as well as a series of drop zones big enough to insert 4,000 men in one drop. A full-scale model town, as large as a city block, is used to hone the paratroopers' urban fighting skills. Overall, training is rugged, realistic, and continuous. In a given year a paratrooper trains nearly 270 days, runs 700 miles, conducts a minimum of 12 parachute operations and participates in several day and night live-fire exercises.

Always On Call

Today, 82nd Division paratroopers are deployed across the globe and are on constant standby. A field artillery regiment, a division support command, and an aviation brigade each support the infantry regiments. In addition, the division has engineer, signal, armour, military intelligence, and air defence battalions, each consisting of more than 400 paratroopers. To support the infantry, the division's inventory also includes M-119 105mm howitzers, the Avenger Air Defence weapon system, which fires the Stinger missile from an eight-missile

The division is supported by OH-58D Kiowa Warrior helicopters armed with an AGM -114 Hellfire and seven Hydra rockets. (US DoD)

The 82nd Aviation Brigade uses both the UH-60 Black Hawk pictured here and the OH-58D Kiowa Warrior. (US DoD)

Chinook helicopters were the workhorse of the 82nd SAB in Iraq and Afghanistan. (US DoD)

pod mounted on a vehicle, the shoulder-fired Stinger missile, and the Sheridan armoured reconnaissance vehicle. The 82nd Aviation Brigade has both the UH-60 Black Hawk and the OH-58D Kiowa Warrior helicopters.

Separate battalions, such as the 307th Engineers, the 82nd Signal and the 313th Military Intelligence, each have their own high-technology equipment that can be employed to provide vital support to the division. Virtually all of the division's weapons and equipment can be delivered by parachute. Sophisticated night-vision equipment is used by 82nd paratroopers to gain command of the battlefield at night. The troops are able to perform their missions as quickly and efficiently under the cover of darkness as they can in broad daylight.

This combination of intensive training, sophisticated weapons, and cutting-edge technology make the 82nd Airborne Division one of the most awesome fighting forces in the world. This division continues to preserve the traditions established in its combat operations. As the contingency division that forms the core of the United States' strategic combat force, the 82nd is always ready to deploy anywhere in the world within 18 hours.

Solders from the 82nd AB on patrol in Mosul in 2003. (US DoD)

A US paratrooper detains an Iraqi suspect during operations around Baghdad. (US DoD)

A Chinook delivers supplies during a training exercise. (US DoD)

The 82nd played a major role in the coalition deployment to Afghanistan after 9/11 and in the invasion of Iraq in 2003., where the division spearheaded major operations in Baghdad, Mosul, and Kirkuk. During the enduring operations against the Taliban the 82nd served across the country, taking the fight directly to the enemy as well as assisting in the training of Afghan National Security Forces (ANSF). Since the end of combat operations in Afghanistan, UK and US airborne units have taken part in annual joint exercises in the US, the UK and into Europe.

In 2018 soldiers from UK's 3rd Battalion the Parachute Regiment joined elements of the 82nd AB flying directly from Fort Bragg, North Carolina, in a fleet of US Air Force C-17 Globemaster transport aircraft, before jumping into the drop zone (DZ) together with heavy equipment including vehicles and vital stores. Speaking moments after landing, Colonel Andrew Jackson, deputy commander of 16 Air Assault Brigade, described the exercise as 'a clear and unmistakable show of airborne strength on a global scale'. He said: "There's a reason why most of the world's reference armies still maintain an airborne capability, because in strategic terms it's not possible to get this many men and this much equipment anywhere on the globe so quickly by any other means. This is a very public statement that the 82nd Airborne Division GRF (Global Response Force), with

A Black Hawk of the 82nd AB Aviation regiment in Zabul, Afghanistan. (US DoD)

82nd Airborne soldiers pictured on operations in Syria in 2022. (US DoD)

16 Brigade as part of it, is able to project significant force at short notice."

In August 2021, elements of the 82nd Airborne Division, including the Immediate Response Force, deployed to Afghanistan to secure the evacuation of American diplomats and Afghan Special Immigrant Visa applicants as the Taliban seized power across the country and converged on Kabul. At the airport they worked alongside British paratroopers in what was a difficult and tense operation as armed insurgents stood watching the American and British troops manage the airlift of more than 100,000 people out of the capital in under 15 days. Today, the Parachute Regiment has forged a Joint Rapid Response capability with the US Army's 82nd Airborne Division (82nd AA) to enhance readiness and strategic reach. This was demonstrated in 2021 when paratroopers from 2 PARA joined the 3rd Brigade Combat Team of the 82nd AB in a Joint Forcible Entry exercise, flying direct from the United States and jumping into Estonia. In May 2023, UK paratroopers jumped alongside US, Czech Republic, Latvian, Polish, and Estonian allies as part of a large-scale American-led military exercise to send a clear message to Moscow of NATO's capability. Soldiers from the UK's 2nd Battalion the Parachute Regiment jumped in darkness with the 82nd AB to secure an airfield from a simulated enemy threat, provided by the Estonian Territorial Defence Force, before preparing to move into a tactical training exercise. ●

A sniper team takes part in night training to hone their skills prior to deployment to Syria. (US DoD)

TODAY

Aeroplane is still providing the best aviation coverage around. With focus on iconic military aircraft from the 1930s to the 1960s.

shop.keypublishing.com/amsubs

Aviation News is renowned for providing the best coverage of every branch of aviation.

shop.keypublishing.com/ansubs

hing.com

NORMANDY 6th AIRBORNE DIVISION

The **6th Airborne Division** spearheaded the assault into Normandy and were the first to set foot on enemy territory on D-Day, landing by parachute and glider soon after midnight on June 6, 1944. Their mission: to seize and hold the bridges across the River Orne and the Caen Canal, to immobilise the guns of the Merville Battery, sever possible routes of a German counterattack and secure the left flank of the invasion. All these objectives were achieved. The coup de main glider borne operations were totally successful, with Pegasus Bridge being the first to be captured by the airborne soldiers of the Oxfordshire & Buckinghamshire Light Infantry.

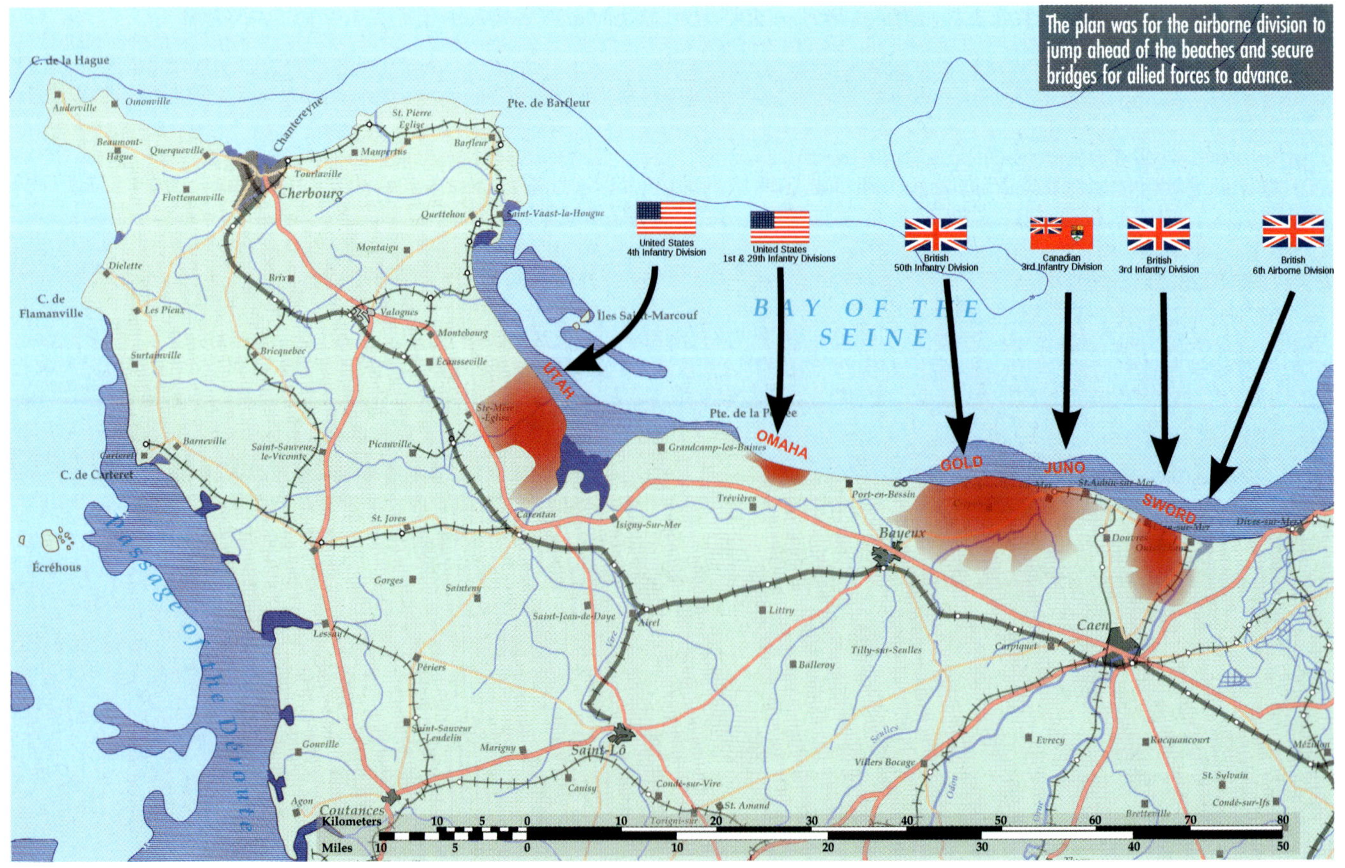

The night sky concealed the anxiety on their young faces as the British paratroopers crowded aboard the Stirling bomber - among them was a teenage soldier, called Robert 'Bobby' Johns . He had run away to join up and fight for his country. Carrying their equipment packs, rifle and parachute the soldiers crammed themselves into the seats, facing each other, ten to a side, with their backs against the cold aluminium of the fuselage. It was 9pm on June 5, 1944, just three hours away from D-Day, when the first paratroopers were expected to jump into France. It was the action that every soldier had been thinking about for the previous two years. Now fully loaded with troops, the long row of planes bearing black and white invasion stripes on their wings and fuselage, lurched forward one after another down the runway at Broadwell Airfield, a Royal Air Force base in Oxfordshire.

Lieutenant Jack Watson commanded a platoon in A Company of the 13th (Lancashire) Parachute Battalion, sat calmly aboard one of the aircraft unaware that ➲

Paratroopers flew to Normandy in a variety of aircraft including Stirling bombers. (War Office)

British paratroopers from 3rd Battalion Parachute Regiment prepare to head for France. (DPL Archives)

one of his men sitting close by, Private Robert 'Bobby' Johns, was about to make history. He would become the youngest soldier to parachute into Normandy, as the 6th Airborne Division spearheaded the invasion of France.

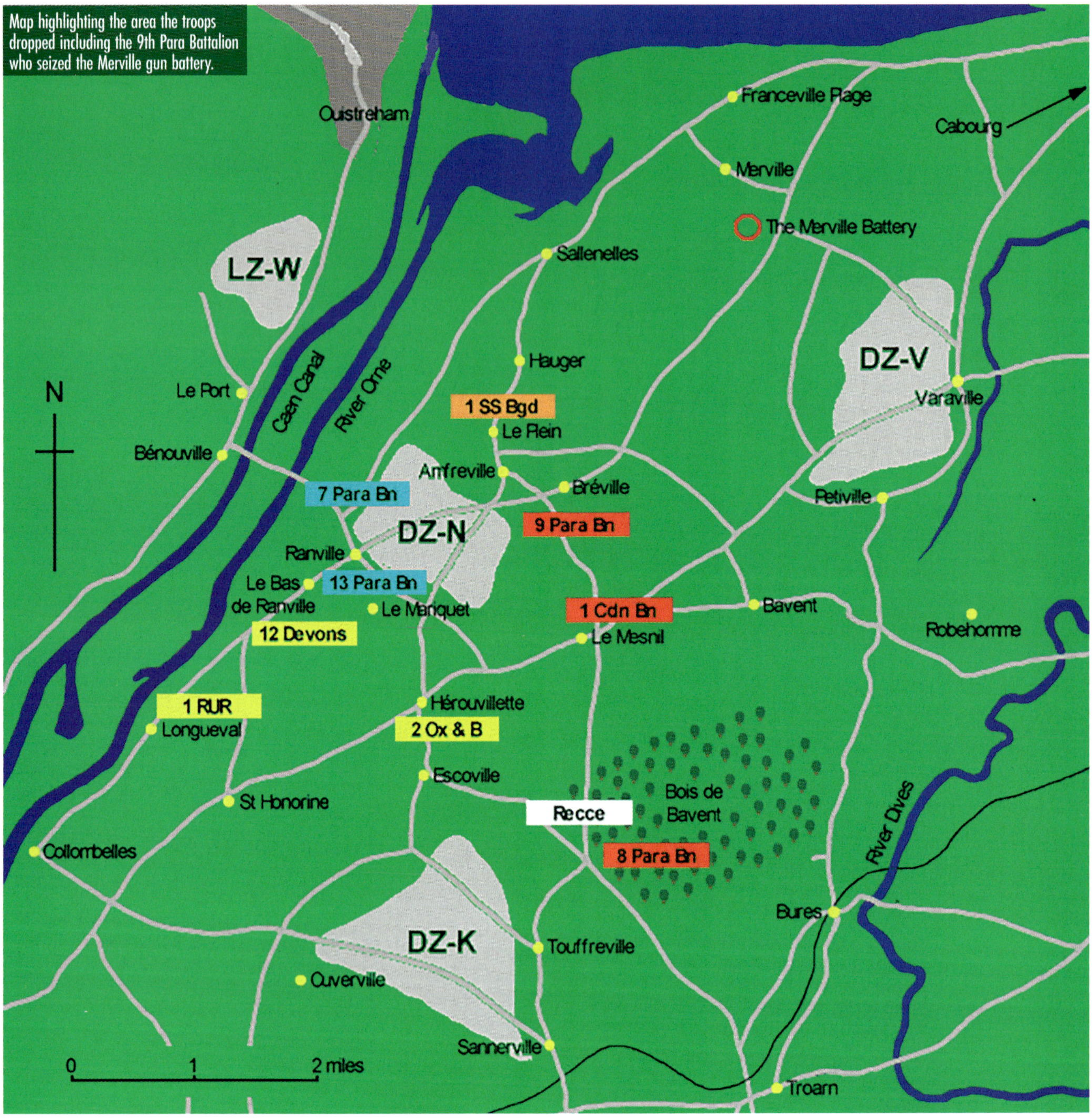

His military record stated that Pte Robert Edward Johns was 18 years old – but he wasn't. He was just 16 – two years below the minimum age for active service. Watson was also unaware that his young charge was the subject of the British Army's own real-life version of the famous film *Saving Private Ryan*. In an echo of the blockbuster Hollywood movie – in which Tom Hank's character searches for the last surviving son of the fictional Ryan family after his brothers are killed in action – Bobby's frantic parents had appealed to the War Office, the police, and the local authority to trace him and enquiries were underway. The couple had already lost one son in the war, and another had been injured.

As their aircraft flew low over the channel, few onboard spoke. It was cold and dark, some

Thousands of soldiers were now being trained in readiness for the airborne assault into Europe. (DPL Archives)

A machine gun team stands ready to be inspected during their readiness for D-Day. (DPL Archives)

tried to sleep, others thought of home while several fought off air sickness. Then just before 1am the order was passed down the line that they were over the French coast and just five minutes from the drop zone. In a well-rehearsed procedure, the RAF parachute instructor signalled the paratroopers to stand up. Watson and his platoon got to their feet and hooked the D-rings attached to their parachute static lines to the overhead wire – a procedure they had done many times in training. This would ensure that as they exited the aircraft their X-Type canopy, then still listed as a top-secret by the war office, would open automatically. The soldiers shuffled towards the exit, their equipment strapped to their left leg, which would hang below them when they exited the aircraft. The RAF instructor grabbed the shoulder of the first man in the 'stick' of 20 soldiers to steady him in the doorway. The first man was often the tallest and heaviest allowing him to drop quickly and not get tangled in the rigging lines of smaller, lighter soldiers behind him. A small box mounted by the door showed two lights, one red and one green. It represented the final stage in a paratroopers' exit from the plane. The first soldier stood in the doorway poised to jump as he watched the red-light light to his left. Suddenly the red light went out and the green bulb flickered on, at the same time the shout came from the RAF parachute instructor Go! Go! Go! The paratroopers were quickly out of the door and into the night sky. Each man checked the sky around him to make sure he was not too close to a colleague and a potential collision. After less than 20 seconds in the air, the soldiers landed on French soil with a thump and a roll.

The huge volume of planes and gliders as well as the German artillery flak caused an element of confusion and resulted in some troops being dropped in the wrong areas and missing their correct drop zones. But the paratroopers and glider troops were now on the ground – it was June 6 and their war had begun. ➲

An RAF instructor checks the webbing straps of a soldier's parachute; extra equipment can be seen bundled under their smocks below the parachute. (DPL Archives)

The Queen escorted by Major General Gale speaks to glider pilots who were bound for Normandy. (DPL Archives)

The Queen meets paratroopers prior to D-Day — the operation was surrounded in secrecy, but the royals visited to raise morale. (DPL Archives)

warrant and instructed to travel to Larkhill in Wiltshire where the battalion was re-roling to become the 13th Battalion of the Parachute Regiment.

He had not discussed his plans to run off and join up with his parents, Henry, and Daisy Johns, who were devastated by his sudden disappearance. His Dad was a crane driver, and his mother was a domestic cleaner. The couple had four children, William, Ronald, Ivor, and Robert, otherwise known as Bobby. Mum and Dad were still mourning the loss of their eldest son, William aged 23, he had been killed when the Luftwaffe bombed his submarine, the Porpoise class HMS *Narwhal* - killing all 59 crew. It had been laying mines off Norway in 1940 when German bombers struck. His brother Ronald had served on HMS *Pembroke* but was discharged after being shot in the eye in a freak accident in 1938. Bobby was the

Robert 'Bobby' Johns

Sixteen-year-old Private Johns had run away from home at just 14 years old and enlisted in the army, hoodwinking the sergeant in his local recruitment office in Portsmouth by claiming he was older. His official army record shows he listed his date of birth as July 25, 1925, and he joined up on June 15, 1943 - initially being assigned to the General Service Corps and sent to Number 22 Primary Training Centre in Derby, England. His medical report shows that he was 5ft 3in tall, weighed 135lb and according to the medical examiner, Doctor Robert Brown, had a fresh complexion and blue eyes. He wanted to join the Royal Electrical Mechanical Engineers, but demand meant that commanders wanted infantry soldiers and he was directed to the Royal Fusiliers. In late 1943 he volunteered for 'specialist service' with Britain's newly created airborne forces and in January 1944 Bobby was ordered to join the South Lancashire Regiment. He was issued with a rail

King Charles III regularly visits France on the anniversary of the D-Day landings. (MOD/Crown Copyright)

youngest of the couple's four children and could not wait to leave the family's home and seek adventure. They lived in a two-bedroom terraced home in Jervis Road, Stramshaw, in the shadow of Portsmouth's naval dockyard. His parents Henry and Daisy Johns were beside themselves with worry when they discovered that Bobby was missing. They had contacted his friends, the police, and the local recruitment office. But no one could shed any light on their son's whereabouts. Nevertheless, his parents lodged an 'underage enlistment' report with the military, just in case he had tried to join up. The paperwork eventually arrived on the desk of an official at the War Office in London. In the 1940s many boys left school at 14 and thousands lied about their age and enlisted. However, the guidelines for the military were clear: underage soldiers should be immediately returned home to the UK and their families.

The War Office had instigated a search for Pte Johns, but locating underage soldiers was not regarded as a priority at a time when men and resources were in short supply. In any case, efficient administration was hampered by the rapid formation and training of new units in secret preparation for D-Day. Bobby's initial unit the 2nd/4th battalion the South Lancashire Regiment was now re-designated to the 13th (Lancashire) Parachute Battalion. At RAF Ringway near Manchester, he joined Course 98 at No 1 Parachute Training School and on January 10, 1944, he began a 12-day course which culminated with him jumping from a balloon and subsequently a Whitley bomber. His course reports state that he was the youngest there and the best performer. But still, no one had questioned his age. Bobby was just 15-years-old when he was awarded his parachute ➲

Parachute drops took place as battalion tested their readiness for D-Day. (DPL Archives)

Major General Gale addresses his soldiers of the 6th Airborne Division before they embark on Operation Overlord, the invasion of Europe. (DPL Archives)

Paratroopers of the 6th Airborne Division climbing into an Armstrong Whitworth Albemarle aircraft at RAF Harwell, June 5, 1944. (DPL Archives)

Glider troops with axes in hand to cut themselves out of their aircraft if it crashed prepare for D-Day. (DPL Archives)

'wings' and presented with his coveted maroon beret. Those who passed the course joined the new 13th Parachute Battalion, which had been officially formed in May 1943, and spent months training soldiers and preparing.

Meanwhile, his parents continued to make enquiries about their son but heard nothing. Nevertheless, the War Office did persist in making checks to trace anyone with the surname 'Johns' who had enlisted in the Portsmouth area. However, routine administrative communications with units preparing for France were far from the top of any 'action' pile of correspondence and replies took weeks or months to come through. As D-Day approached, Bobby and his comrades in A Company went into isolation at a camp near RAF Broadwell in Oxfordshire, ready to carry out final preparations prior to being called forward to board their aircraft. These aircraft would soon roar over Bobby's home in Portsmouth and take them to war.

The assault forces are in the sky, heading for France as the allowed invasion of Europe commences. (DPL Archives)

Some paratroopers found themselves on the wrong drop zones, but they quickly collated themselves and moved towards their objectives. (DPL Archives)

Private Bobby Johns had joined the 13th Battalion and was the youngest man to jump on D-Day – just 16 years old. (DPL Archives)

asparagus' proved much easier. We then waited for the gliders to arrive, bringing in Major General Richard Gale, his staff, and some much-needed anti-tank guns. At 0315 hours they started to come in, but not from the north as expected. They appeared from all directions. It was a nightmare, and extremely frightening. I would rather be shelled any day! Some landed well, others crashed into each other. The sparks from the skids, the sounds of splintering wood, and the yells from the ➲

On French Soil

Within minutes of landing on French soil, the 13th Battalion's hunting horn was sounding – this was used as a rallying call and soldiers headed towards the sound to form up with their company. Lieutenant Watson landed to find himself all alone. He later recalled: "I took off with from RAF Broadwell at 2330 hours. In the Channel, I could see below me ships signalling 'V' for Victory. Our battalion's task was to secure Ranville and to protect the DZ (drop zone) and LZ (landing zone) for the gliders. As I landed my parachute got caught up in the trees, so I had a fairly soft landing. I was lucky, but I was alone! I collected my equipment together and saw Ranville church tower and made for it, meeting my men on the way. The DZ was a real bugger's muddle, with all three battalions of our Brigade landing and some sticks of the 8th Battalion, who had been dropped on the wrong DZ, it was all mixed up. But the hunting horns sounded clearly, and when I reached the rendezvous, the company was about 40 strong - half an hour later, we were up to 60. I was missing one section and my platoon sergeant. While we were clearing the area, we could hear the fighting going on at Ranville, which our battalion captured by 0230 hours, the first village to be captured in France".

The Germans had covered fields with large poles, dubbed asparagus by the Brits, and dug ditches to damage aircraft and deter any landings. Lt Watson added: "Despite heavy mortaring and machine-gun fire, the poles were removed, and the ditches filled in by 0300 hours. The poles were, fortunately, not as large as expected. We had trained to remove telegraph poles, and the so called 'Rommel's

A Horsa glider is lifted into the air bound for France, it was glider borne soldiers from the Oxford and Buckinghamshire Light Infantry who seized Pegasus Bridge. (DPL Archives)

Glider troops send a message to Hitler and remember their girlfriends' and wives' names on the fuselage of their Horsa glider. (DPL Archives)

The Royal Artillery Air Landing units packed howitzers aboard their gliders. (War Office)

Glider pilots make a final check of the map before setting off for Normandy in June 1944. (War Office)

Pegasus Bridge captured and held by the British – a glider which had delivered the troops who seized it can be seen in the background. (War Office)

occupants, was like a scene from hell. Some of our men were hit by debris and it was a miracle that the occupants of these smashed up gliders then got out".

Ranville

Dug in around the rubble and the ruins of Ranville, the 13th Battalion was subjected to constant artillery and mortar bombardments and sporadic infantry assaults for 11 successive days before the 1st Canadian Parachute Battalion arrived to relieve them. The second in command of A Company, Captain Harry Ainsworth, broke his leg when they parachuted onto drop zone 'N', and Watson was promoted to the rank of captain in his place. He later wrote in his report: "On the morning of D+4 (four days after D-Day) patrols from our battalion reported signs of movement as if the enemy were preparing to attack. At about 0900 hrs our forward positions reported that the enemy were moving across the DZ and LZs using the mass of wrecked gliders as cover and were heading towards the direction of the battalion position – we were ready for them. The enemy were allowed to come within 50 yards of the battalion line when the order was given to fire. The result was devastating – the enemy were falling like a house of cards. They suffered 400 dead or wounded, and we took some 150 prisoners and passed them back to

Soldiers unload a jeep and trailer from a Horsa glider. (War Office)

RAF parachute packers prepared thousands of chutes for the Normandy assault. (War Office)

the brigade holding area. They were a German Grenadier Battalion of 346 Division. We lost quite a few men through shelling, but we held our ground and eventually, we were moved to Le Mesnil to take over the 3rd Parachute Brigade position." Above the village of Putot-en-Auge, there was an enormous hill called Hill 13, which was heavily defended by the Germans. The paras fought hard to take it and succeeded but were then forced back by the Nazis who outnumbered them. Eventually, 48 Commando of the 4th Special Service Brigade arrived and supported an assault which captured the hill.

At the War Office, Bobby's case had been investigated by army officers and finally, they had discovered his location – he was with the 13th Parachute Battalion. The investigating officer wrote to Lieutenant Colonel Peter Luard, the commanding officer of Bobby's battalion to confirm that Private Johns, regimental number 14434704, was in France. Once his location was established a team from the Royal Military Police was sent to bring him back. A letter was sent to Henry and Daisy Johns informing them that their son had been found and was serving in France. Tragically, however, the search for Bobby would not have a happy Hollywood ➲

Two Hamilcar gliders land in Normandy, they could carry light vehicles and field guns as well as soldiers. (War Office)

Private Johns, back row fifth from the right pictured with soldiers from A Company, 13th Parachute Battalion just before D-Day. (DPL Archives)

A Dakota drops paratroopers over Normandy in an annual airborne remembrance of D-Day. (DPL Archives)

Soldiers of the modern-day Parachute Regiment watch colleagues jump at a Normandy anniversary to remember those who made the ultimate sacrifice in June 1944. (DPL Archives)

Horsa gliders, many of which appear to have made a safe landing, are left abandoned in Normandy. (DPL Archives)

The grave stone of Private Robert 'Bobby' Johns who died on July 23, 1944, aged just 16. (DPL Archives)

The memorial stone at Ranville to remember the 13th Battalion, who Private Bobby Johns served with. (DPL Archives)

ending. On reaching his unit, Military Police officers discovered that Bobby had been killed in action on July 23, 1944, at Le Mesnil, a month before his 17th birthday. It was recorded by the battalion that a sniper had shot him close to Le Mesnil crossroads. Bobby Johns was buried in July 1944 at Ranville war cemetery and his headstone bears his age, 16-years-old and the inscription 'He lived as he died, fearlessly'.

Shortly before Jack Watson who finished his service with the rank of major passed away in 2011, he said: "The fighting was intense. We were at the forefront of the main effort to prevent a German counterattack. It was only when he died that we found out his real age.

I remember him well; he was very capable and ready to help. He was fearless. He loved being a paratrooper and I never suspected that he was underage. When we were informed that he was just 16, I was shocked and very sad." The war diary for the 13th Battalion on July 23, 1944 – the day Bobby Johns was killed – recorded that: "The enemy was very sensitive all day and fired on the least provocation. C Company were, unfortunately, sustaining a number of casualties from enemy mortar fire as a result of very accurate fire from 50mm and 81mm mortars on their forward positions. Two casualties were also caused by enemy sniper fire." One of them was Bobby Johns. ●

A glider pilot makes a perfect landing other than losing his front wheel. (US Army Library)

ARNHEM
A BRIDGE TOO FAR

Allied paratroopers jump into Arnhem on September 17 every year to mark
the anniversary of Operation Market Garden in 1944. (DPL Archives)

After D-Day, the Germans were in retreat and General Montgomery proposed an ambitious operation to seize and hold a bridgehead over the Lower Rhine River. Its objective was to push 60 miles into German territory, creating an Allied invasion route into northern Germany. Two American divisions, the British 1st Airborne Division and the 1st Polish Parachute Brigade, were assigned to the task which would see an airborne carpet of paratroopers and glider-borne troops dropped into Holland. The British, commanded by Major-General Roy Urquhart, was ordered to take the bridge at Arnhem. The mission failed when ground forces could not link up with them — but the Paras fought a heroic rear-guard action which has entered the annals of military history.

The battle for Arnhem had been planned as the spearhead of a powerful Allied thrust through Holland and across the Rhine, using a massive airborne force to jump ahead of the ground troops to secure the route. Field Marshal Bernard Montgomery launched Operation Market Garden with the objective of laying an 'airborne carpet' across Holland, over which the Allies could stream into Germany and shorten the war by months. General Sir Frederick 'Boy' Browning commanded the 1st Airborne Corps, and his plan involved the capture of five major river and canal crossings, with Arnhem as the ultimate prize of what was to be a bridgehead into Hitler's heartland. Two American formations were assigned to the crossings farther south - the 101st Airborne at Eindhoven and the 82nd Airborne at Grave and Nijmegen. At the end of the line, at Arnhem, were the 1st British Airborne Division and the 1st Polish Parachute Brigade. After they had captured the bridge, Browning's plan was that armoured columns of 30 Corps and other units, would dash 60 miles across the flat Dutch terrain and link up with the airborne units, before the enemy had chance to reinforce their defences.

Weather pending, the jump was scheduled to take place on September 17, 1944, with 10,000 Allied paratroopers filling the skies above Holland, unaware of the troubled times ahead of them and the fact that fewer than 3,000 would return. The concept was bold and simple, but it lacked aircraft and the Polish brigade were still on the ground in England four days after the assault began. Intelligence warnings of heavy concentrations of battle-hardened German Panzer troops were ignored or underestimated, and 10,000 of Britain's best troops, lightly armed, were landed miles from their objective, to be cut to pieces with little hope of escape or reinforcement. By September 17, when the landings began, there were detailed reports from a well-organised Dutch Resistance that

The skies over Arnhem filled with parachutes as the 1st Airborne Division arrived on September 17, 1944. (DPL Archives)

The skies over Dutch local towns filled with the aircraft as they made their way to Arnhem. (DPL Archives)

Wave after wave of planes dropped paratroopers, but a shortage of aircraft delayed some units. (DPL Archives)

An RAF aerial shot of the airborne landings in Holland in September 1944. (War Office)

Field Marshall Montgomery planned that Operation Market Garden would allow the Allies to punch a path across the Rhine. (War Office)

General Sir Frederick 'Boy' Browning was later accused of ignoring intelligence about the strength of the German units in Arnhem. (War Office)

many thousands of trained German troops had withdrawn into the area as the Allies extended their D-Day successes. There were warnings of an estimated 70,000 troops with 400 guns, and of major SS armoured formations in the area. General Browning was also warned that the Rhine crossing could only be secured by major landings north and south of the bridge, preceded by a glider assault of the style which had proved so brilliantly successful at the Pegasus Bridge in Normandy. It is clear from the diaries of Major General Gale that General Browning consulted him about the Arnhem plan. Gale made it clear that he needed to land the whole division close to the bridge and mount a coup de main drop to spring surprise at Arnhem bridge itself. Browning asked Gale what he would do if pressed to accept the plan. Gale was clear. "Then sir, I should resign."

Ignored 'Intelligence'

Allied intelligence reports had also suggested that German morale was low and enemy forces in the area were weak, but nothing could have been further from the truth. German spirits were, in fact, high, and an SS panzer unit was in Arnhem, overhauling its tanks. The Germans ➲

Major General Urquhart outside his headquarters in Arnhem. (War Office)

At Ringway and other bases training was now focussed on generating more paratroopers for the 1st Airborne Division. (DPL Archives)

with Bren-gun and rifle fire. Frost decided to make a dash for the main road bridge. By dusk his men were barricading themselves into buildings on either side of its northern approach ramp. If his military superiors had indeed been warned of the likely presence of German panzer units, this vital information was evidently not passed down to him or his company commanders. Years later he confided to another veteran survivor at a reunion that he had been led to expect to face lightly armed infantry troops. Lt Col Frost, who had led the attack on Bruneval and had seen action all over north Africa and Sicily, had against all odds, reached his objective. He later wrote: "The whole idea of parachutists was that they should land behind the enemy, and not be forced to cross rivers in the face of intense fire." Earlier, before flying out to lead his battalion, Frost had ordered his golf clubs to be packed so he could enjoy himself after beating the Germans, but the Nazis had other ideas. To repulse the Paras' advance, they poured more SS troops into

were initially taken by surprise and after the Paras landed at Renkum Common, eight miles west of Arnhem, the 1st Parachute Brigade set off in the direction of their objective - to seize the road and rail bridges across the Rhine. Led by Lieutenant Colonel Frost, the 2nd Battalion took the lower Oosterbeek road heading for Arnhem bridge, while the 1st and 3rd Battalions took separate routes in the same direction, only to be ambushed by German armoured units. The Germans quickly realised what was happening, and fighting began along the roadside. One of the first to lose his life was Major General Kussin, the local German field commander and Arnhem town commandant. His camouflaged Citroen staff car was speeding down the road from Wolfheze when the driver realised, too late, that he was heading straight into the leading platoons of British soldiers. As the car skidded to a halt it was riddled

Parachuting was now taking place every day as commanders prepared the force for Market Garden. (DPL Archives)

The King inspects jeeps which were destined be flown to Arnhem aboard gliders. (DPL Archives)

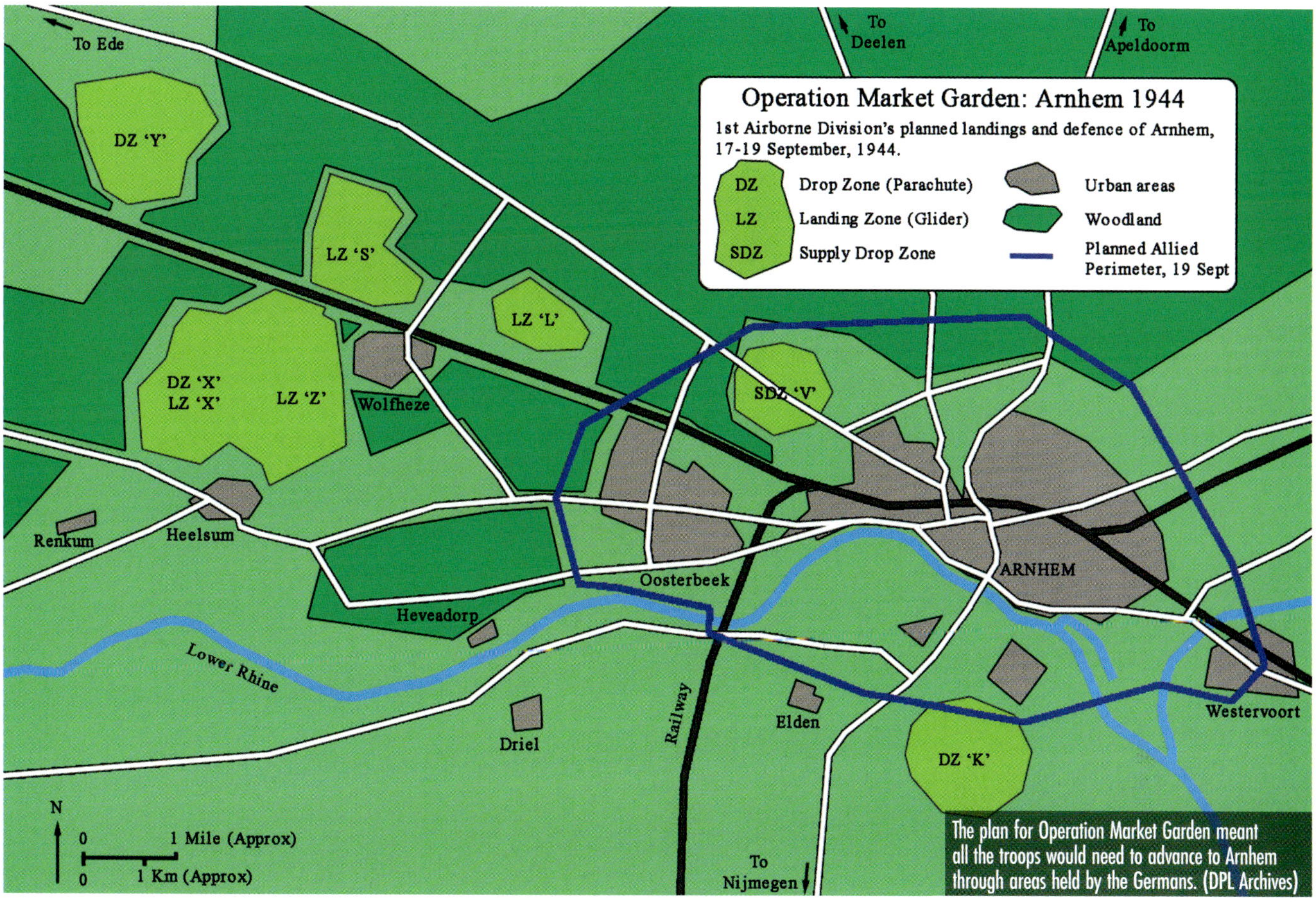

The plan for Operation Market Garden meant all the troops would need to advance to Arnhem through areas held by the Germans. (DPL Archives)

Arnhem, including three crack panzer units, supported by heavy armour. Frost, like the other battalion commanders, had been told that they only had to defend the bridge for 48 hours until 30 Corps arrived. But the ground troops failed in their task and the Paras were left to face a bitter fight against German armour on their own. At dawn on September 18, Frost's Paras were rushed by a force of five armoured and

There were several variants of glider, but none offered much room for troops. (War Office)

As at D-Day, glider borne troops made a significant contribution to the operation. (War Office)

seven tracked troop carriers, in an attempt by the Germans to take the bridge. All the vehicles were knocked out with anti-tank weapons. They burned all day under the eyes of the Paras and their enemy, blocking the bridge until the end of the battle. The Germans made repeated attempts to cross the bridge from the south, at such close quarters that British troops were able to drop grenades into passing half-tracks from bedroom windows.

Lieutenant John Grayburn VC

Lieutenant John Grayburn led one of the patrols which had to be sent into the teeth of the German defences in an attempt to secure the southern approach to the bridge. Almost immediately Grayburn was wounded in the shoulder as his platoon was met by a blizzard of shells from two quick-firing 20mm cannons and machine guns from armoured cars. Still, he pressed forward until his casualties became so heavy, he was ordered to withdraw. He came off the bridge, where there was no chance of cover, only when he was sure that the last survivors of his men were safe. He then set about creating a strongpoint in a house which was to prove decisive in holding back the enemy. It was exposed to several fields of fire, and became the target of ceaseless attacks from infantry, mortars, and heavy machine guns, and finally tanks and self-propelled artillery. His men held out only because he ➲

Polish paratroopers meeting the deputy Prime Minister Clement Attlee during training. They became part of the 1st Airborne Division that jumped at Arnhem. (Home Office)

himself ignored the danger and moved among them with words of encouragement when it mattered most. Against all odds he and his men held out for two days and left their positions only when the house was burning about their heads. Still suffering from his wounds, the young lieutenant gathered the survivors of his company and any man in the area who could still fight. He organised them into a combat unit which, to the astonishment of the enemy, began to launch a series of attacks. Instead of the quick kill they must have expected, the Germans found themselves the targets of such aggressive fighting patrols that they had to call up heavy tanks.

Lt Grayburn saw German engineers laying demolition charges under the bridge, which he knew was vital to the Allied advance, and

Paratroopers of the 1st Parachute battalion fighting around Arnhem. (DPL Archives)

A still from the film *A Bridge too Far*, gives a colourful perspective idea of the devastation fighting endured by the men of 2nd battalion Parachute Regiment. (Joseph E Levine Productions)

drove the Nazis back long enough to remove the fuses. He was again badly wounded, this time in his back, but again he waved away attempts to get him to an aid station. He fought on until faced with a heavy tank, against which his tiny group now had no defence. This time he was put under direct orders to pull back and stood in full view of the panzer crew to direct his survivors to what remained of Colonel Frost's defensive perimeter. Grayburn was killed that night, after three days in constant combat. He was later awarded the Victoria Cross, his citation stated: "For over three days, Lieutenant Grayburn led his men with supreme gallantry and determination. Though in pain, weakened by wounds, short of food and without sleep, his courage never flagged.

A still from the film *A Bridge too Far*, shows the armour vehicles that the paras faced. (Joseph E Levine Productions)

Lieutenant Colonel John Frost who commanded the 2nd Battalion Parachute Regiment at Arnhem and was himself captured.

Victor Gregg who served with the 10th Battalion the Parachute Regiment. (DPL Archives)

There is no doubt that, but for this officer's inspiring leadership and personal bravery, the Arnhem Bridge could never have been held for this time."

On the third day of the battle, a short truce had allowed the wounded to be taken into German captivity. Then the fighting resumed, until one by one the Paras having fired every round in their possession were overrun; just 100 men remained. After the battle, in which the Paras won five Victoria Crosses, the American General Dwight Eisenhower was full of praise for the airborne warriors. He said: "There has been no single performance by any unit that has more greatly inspired me or more excited my admiration than the nine-day action by the 1st British Parachute Division between September 17 – 25".

A total of 10,095 had dropped by parachute or glider into Holland but by the end of the battle 7,578 were listed as killed, wounded, or missing.

Victor Gregg was one of 582 Paras of the 10th Battalion the Parachute Regiment who dropped into Holland. While the

Lieutenant Jack Grayburn who transferred to the Paras and won a Victoria Cross at Arnhem. (War Office)

A mortar crew from the South Staffordshire's pictured during heavy fighting around Arnhem (DPL Archives)

Paratroopers test their communications equipment after arriving in Holland, many radios did not work. (War Office)

initial drop on September 17 faced light opposition, by the time the 10th Battalion landed on the second day (September 18) a German SS unit was waiting for them and over the following days his battalion fought to virtual annihilation. Before they dropped, they had formed up at the village of Somerby in Leicestershire where they waited for their turn to lift off from RAF Spanhoe in a fleet of Dakota aircraft and flew across the channel to Holland - jumping 64 miles behind enemy lines. Speaking before his death Vic said: "As we approached the drop-zone I think we were all quietly anxious, the Germans were firing at us and as we jumped some chaps were shot dead in the sky, it was awful. They were young lads who had hardly had a chance to experience life. The Germans had an armoured force waiting for us and as we got on the ground, I could hear lads who were wounded screaming, it was bedlam. Blokes were running around to find their mates and moving to forming up points on the drop

Airborne troops dug in around Oosterbeek. (DPL Archives).

A soldier displays the clothing and weapons the Paras would have worn at Arnhem. (War Office)

zone, but the Germans were relentless and many of our men were killed where they landed. I had the heavy machine gun, so I couldn't just run off the drop zone, so me and my mates took cover and assembled it, we kept our heads down and I think that saved our lives. But the days that followed were horrendous, we were almost wiped out. We quickly ran out of ammunition and food, and we were forced to take supplies from those who had passed away, just to make sure we could continue the fight against the Germans. By day six my two mates on the gun with me were dead, we were exhausted, out of ammunition and finally captured and taken off to a prisoner of war camp, we did our best"

The Ardennes

Three months after Arnhem in December 1944, the German armies launched a massive counter attack through the forests of the Ardennes. The Nazi plan was aimed

British soldiers from the 1st Airborne Division taken prisoner of war. (War Office)

A captured airborne officer shares a joke with his men. (War Office)

at splitting the Allied forces and pushing through a German advance fast and furious. Montgomery called for reinforcements and the 6th Airborne division, recently rested after their success in Normandy, were ordered to move at once and form a defensive line at crossing points on the River Meuse. The enemy advance was quickly halted, but the Germans re-grouped at Bure and on January 13, 1945, the men of 13 Para were ordered to attack the village. By early 1945 the Allies were closing in on Germany, but the Rhine was a formidable natural obstacle to the Allied advance. Commanders now sought to breach the Rhine in several areas to ensure that the operation was a success, Montgomery insisted that an airborne component be inserted into the plans for the operation, to support the amphibious assaults that would take place; this was code-named Operation Varsity. In total, six parachute battalions, including the Canadians, of the 6th Airborne Division, supported by glider troops from the Air Landing Brigade, dropped on March 24, 1945, as a complete force, avoiding the mistakes of Arnhem. Together with the US 17th Airborne Division, the aim of the operation was to secure and deepen the bridgehead east of the Rhine and then advance across country to the Baltic coast, a journey of 350 miles. Their initial objectives were the high ground overlooking the crossing point at Diers-fordter Wald and the road and rail bridges over the River Issel at Hamminkeln. Flying in tight formation, 540 American Dakota aircraft carried the 12 parachute battalions, five British, one Canadian and six from the US, closely followed by 1,300 gliders, packed with 16,000 troops.

Paratroopers arrive in Hamminkeln on March 25, 1945.

Modern day paratroopers from the 2nd Battalion march over Arnhem bridge to pay their respects to those who made the ultimate sacrifice in September 1944. (DPL Archives)

Every September, school children in Arnhem lay flowers at the British cemetery to remember those who died fighting to liberate their country. (DPL Archives)

A veteran remembers fallen colleagues at Arnhem cemetery. (DPL Archives)

By the end of the first day's action 1,078 men of the 6th Airborne Division had been either killed or wounded, with 50 aircraft and 11 gliders shot down. Weather for the drop was perfect and almost everyone landed on their respective DZ, although some ended up in the trees and were cut down by German machine guns as they fought to free themselves. Within 24 hours, all objectives for the brigade had been achieved and as planned, the division was joined by ground forces of the 21st Army Group, for the advance across Germany. The bridges over the river were secured and the village of Hamminkeln captured, all objectives had been achieved within a day. Field Marshal Montgomery, who was by now the Colonel Commandant of the Parachute Regiment, wanted the 6th Airborne to head the advance and they did so on foot.

On May 5, 1945, General Urquhart was warned to prepare to move his airborne men to Norway, where they were to ensure that the Germans observed the terms of the surrender. For the Paras it was yet another dangerous job. There were 35,000 Germans and just 6,000 airborne troops to monitor them. Later, the 1st Airborne Division was withdrawn to the UK and disbanded on August 26, 1945 - almost four years to the day after its formation. ●

POST-WAR OPERATIONS

The Parachute Regiment mounted its **first post-war operational jump** in 1956. They were dropped into Egypt, after politicians had resorted to military action following the nationalisation of the Franco-British Suez Canal Company by the then President, Colonel Gamal Abdel Nasser. He believed that in only five years the tolls collected from ships passing through the Suez Canal would pay for the construction of the Aswan Dam project. Nasser's actions were seen as a threat to both British and French interests in the region. The two countries agreed that if no progress could be made at the negotiating table, they would send a force to occupy the canal and, if necessary, overthrow Nasser.

The Suez Canal remains a strategic trade route to Europe and when President Nasser nationalised the waterway it resulted in military action. (Suez Canal Co)

Since the end of the war the Paras had continued on operations and the 6th Airborne Division had been sent to Palestine in 1945 as an integral part of the Imperial Strategic Reserve for the Middle East. They soon found themselves deployed to the streets of Tel Aviv and Haifa on internal security, as violence flared between Arab and Jewish communities. With the holocaust over, thousands of Jews sought refuge in Palestine, but a British White Paper, drawn up in 1939, had limited Jewish immigration to 75,000, a figure which was soon exhausted. To the Jews, the decision by the British to impose a restriction on the number of people entering their 'homeland', was inhuman and could only lead to conflict, with extremist groups committed to armed attacks against the security forces. For the Paras it was an unbelievable situation; only months earlier their actions had helped to liberate the Jewish prisoners of war, now they were being spat at and insulted by the same people. In November 1945, Jews in Tel Aviv organised a huge riot in a bid to discredit the Paras and make them appear the oppressors. There were several terrorist groups, of which the Stern gang later became prominent as the most violent and along with others, began to ambush police patrols using 'hit and run' tactics. Bitterness deepened when the Stern gang shot dead seven paratroopers of 5th Parachute Battalion, gunning them down in cold blood. The Jews hated the Red Berets and labelled them anti-Semitic, as well as calling them Kalionets, their word for poppy - a red flower with a black heart. No paratrooper enjoyed Palestine. As one officer recalled: "It was very unrewarding and unreal for soldiers, most of whom had taken part in heavy fighting

President Nasser wanted to use the toll revenue from the Suez Canal to fund a dam, but his actions were a threat to both British and French interests in the region. (Egyptian State)

A corporal of the 6th Airborne Division carries an Austro-Hungarian Schwarzlose machine gun from a chicken shed after a hidden cache of weapons was found in the Jewish settlement of Doroth near Gaza. (War Office)

Soldiers of the 6th Airborne Division greet returning Jews to Haifa. Weeks later they were attacking the Paras. On July 22, 1946, Irgun fighters bombed the King David Hotel in Jerusalem, killing over 90 people, including five paratroopers. (DPL Archives)

Paratroopers enforce a curfew in Tel Aviv after the King David Hotel had been bombed. (National Library of Israel)

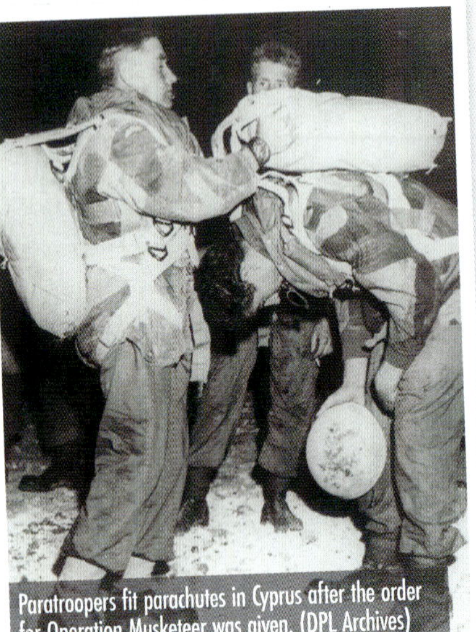

Paratroopers fit parachutes in Cyprus after the order for Operation Musketeer was given. (DPL Archives)

to the Indian Ocean by way of the Red Sea, it allows goods to be shipped between Europe and Asia more directly. It was, and remains, a vital artery of maritime trade and is seen as a strategic waterway. On July 27, 1956, Britain began to prepare an invasion force which, when combined with two French divisions from Algeria, would number 80,000 men. Then on

across Europe and then to find themselves being attacked by these people, that they had helped. It should not be forgotten that the actions of airborne troops helped to secure the liberation of many Jews, yet they suddenly turned on us, I think that is what hurt most. So much of their hatred was directed at the soldier in the red beret. Yet we were not violent with them, in fact we went out of our way to calm situations."

After Palestine, airborne forces were subjected to a major reformation, which also decimated the number of RAF transport aircraft and reduced the force to one single parachute brigade being retained, comprising the 1st, 2nd, and 3rd Battalions. It was named the 16th Independent Parachute Brigade, in respect of the wartime roles of the 1st Airborne and 6th Airborne Divisions, whose numbers formed the title of the new unit.

By early 1956 the Egyptian issue had still not been resolved. At 120 miles long, the Suez Canal connects the Mediterranean Sea

August 2, more than 20,000 British reservists were called up, primarily to help provide the logistic support that such a force would need. The 3rd Battalion had been ordered to prepare for operations, but the exact mission remained secret. The battalion was withdrawn to the UK for training and was issued with the US 106mm anti-tank weapon. Due to the acute shortage of transport aircraft, the invasion of Egypt was based on an amphibious assault timed for November 6, the earliest the ships could arrive, and supported by relatively few parachute troops. The 3rd Battalion Parachute Regiment was selected for the British airborne role, the remainder of the brigade going by sea. At the last moment, the airborne assault was advanced 24 hours depriving the paratroopers of supporting fire from the ships, though naval strike aircraft were to be on call. The airborne plan was for the Paras to secure El Gamil airfield, west of Port Said, for future use, clear the coastal defences between the airfield and the town, and then link with the seaborne Royal Marine Commandos.

The strip of land at El Gamil where the British airborne assault took place. (DPL Archives)

Air strikes by French and British aircraft hit Suez as the parachute assault went in but the naval gunfire was delayed. (DPL Archives)

The main assault lands at El Gamil where Egyptian forces had tried to block the drop zone. (DPL Archives)

soldier was late out of the door and parachuted into the sea. It was decided to jump without reserve parachutes because of the additional weight. This was not a significant decision as reserves had not been used by British airborne forces during World War Two and many of the paratroopers had trained without reserves, which had only recently been introduced.

Invasion

P-Hour was at 0715 GMT and the paratroopers were under fire as soon as they emerged. It had originally been planned to carry out the parachute assault under cover of naval gunfire with the amphibious landings, but as the drop had been brought forward – there was no naval gunfire support. Despite intense ground fire the battalion was on the ground in ten minutes. They began to roll up the Egyptian coastal defences in preparation for the amphibious assault expected the next day. A Company quickly went into action at the west end of the airfield and took the control

A total of 18 Valetta and seven Hastings transport aircraft enabled 668 paratroopers of Lieutenant Colonel Paul Crook's 3rd Battalion to jump. A further seven Hastings aircraft were configured for the heavy drop role, bringing in jeeps, anti-tank recoilless guns, and heavy equipment. The drop zone was on a narrow coastal strip bounded by the Mediterranean to the north and Lake El Manzala to the south, immediately to the west of Port Said. There was scant margin for error. Personal container loads were incredibly heavy with many signallers and mortar base-plate crews carrying equipment weighing more than their own body weight. This caused particular problems in the Valetta aircraft because five people in the stick had to lift their loads over the wing span inside the fuselage, which slowed the exit rate at the end of the stick. As a result, one unfortunate

The commanding officer of 3 Para walks across the drop zone at El Gamil with his command team. (DPL Archives)

Paratroopers landed troops on the drop zone and immediate faced enemy fire. (DPL Archives)

tower and knocked out a bunker firing onto the drop zone. C Company was in the middle of the sticks and provided a battalion reserve. The last to jump was B Company, which captured the east end of the drop zone and was soon engaged in intense fighting to clear the area in and around a sewage farm.

A Parachute Regiment sergeant, who was one of the first out of the door at Suez, still remembers his concern for the unexpected and said: "We were nervous, nobody really

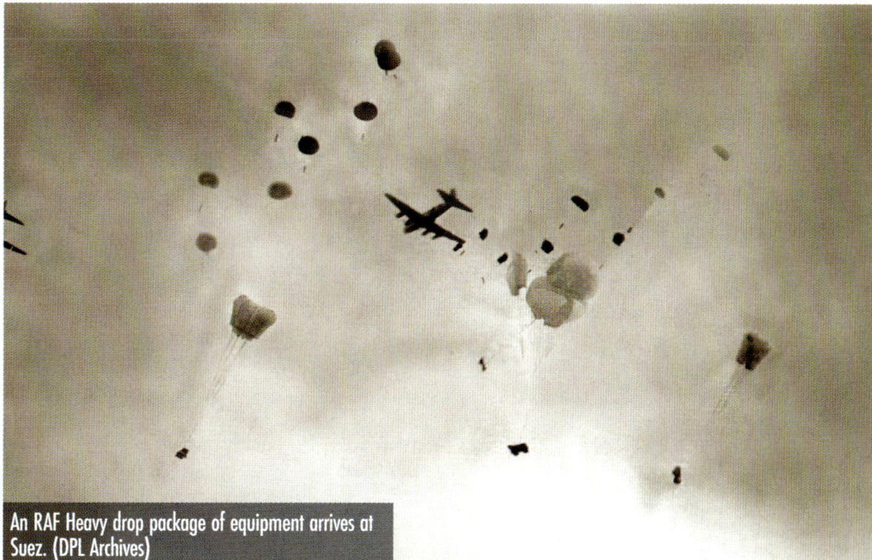

An RAF Heavy drop package of equipment arrives at Suez. (DPL Archives)

Soldiers unpack the 'heavy drop' which included jeeps and trailers. (DPL Archives)

A second wave of Paras is dropped in Suez. (DPL Archives)

The CO during the Suez operation was Lieutenant Colonel Paul Crook seen here with his command team. (DPL Archives)

been announced and the regiment pulled out, heading back to Cyprus. World opinion had forced Britain and France to withdraw their forces. The battalion had acted in the highest traditions of the Parachute Regiment, but the regiment had not been prepared for the operation and new equipment was desperately needed.

Many and Varied Postings

Elsewhere, trouble was now flaring in the Far East. Between 1948 and 1956, communist

knew what to expect, but as soon as we left the aircraft, they started firing at us. The airfield was covered with oil drums to stop aircraft landing and once we had cleared it, we made our way to Port Said. There was quite a bit of fighting, and we took a few injuries, but nothing to shout about."

Meanwhile, French troops with part of the 1st (Guards) Independent Parachute Company, were to capture two vital bridges leading south from Port Said, isolate the town, and exploit down the canal. The odds against parachute soldiers were estimated at five to one. The drop onto the defended airfield achieved initial surprise and, despite flak causing damage to the aircraft and some casualties in the air, the first lift was on the ground in ten minutes. The Egyptian defenders recovered quickly, reacting with vigorous fire from artillery, multi-barrelled rocket launchers, machine guns, mortars, and small arms. Corporal Tony Lowe, who jumped at Suez, said: "The drop itself was over very quickly, we'd flown in at 600 feet, the lowest we could go, and with all the extra weight I was carrying I was soon on the ground. I remember seeing the sand spitting up around my feet at the Egyptians fired at us."

A second smaller lift arrived at 1315 with two Vallettas and five Hastings bringing in D Company and more ammunition. The drop was completed, and the airfield was captured within 30 minutes. The 3rd Battalion lost four men and three officers, and 29 men wounded in the assault and subsequent fighting at Port Said.

The 2nd Battalion came ashore, along with heavy armour, but within a week a ceasefire had

Paratroopers from 3 Para man a security post at Suez. (DPL Archives)

A Royal Tank Regiment Centurion comes ashore at Suez. (DPL Archives)

The British base at Radfan, north of Aden, where the Paras operated from. (DPL Archives)

terrorists had infiltrated Malaya, dominating the jungle terrain and 'brain-washing' whole communities. General Sir Geoffrey Bourne recommended that a Parachute battalion be invited to supply a force of volunteers to fight in the jungle. The War Office agreed, and 80 officers and men of the Parachute Regiment formed the Independent Parachute Squadron and served with distinction until April 1957, when they sailed home on the SS *Nevasa*. In Cyprus, terrorist attacks by the so called EOKA group resulted in the 2nd Battalion remaining on the island in 1957. A year later, 16 Parachute Brigade was flown to Cyprus at short notice as a staging point after civil war broke out in Lebanon. In the event, American forces went in, but within days King Hussein of Jordan had asked Britain for assistance following a coup in Iraq which threatened Jordan. The brigade was flown into Amman to secure the airport and support the King; they remained there for three months. Their presence alone had averted further trouble.

In June 1961, the Paras joined their cousins in the Royal Marines as a deterrent force, deployed on the border of Kuwait, after Iraq threatened to invade the oil rich country. Again, their presence was enough to avoid conflict and for the next six years, until 1967, parachute

A Parachute Regiment patrol pursues a terrorist (DPL Archives)

Paratroopers on patrol in Crater, which became a notorious area for attacks. (DPL Archives)

RAF Bristol Belvedere HC.1, based at Khormaksar, Aden, delivers supplies and mail to a remote location in the mountainous Radfan area of the country. (DPL Archives)

Armoured vehicles deployed in support of the Paras at Sheikh Othman. (DPL Archives)

Rioters in the Crater district of Aden. (DPL Archives)

The regiment deployed to Malaya operating in the jungle. (DPL Archives)

battalions were to be based in the Persian Gulf as a 'fire brigade' force, to react to any conflict in the region. It was also the first time the Paras had been able to take their wives and families with them, based in sunny Bahrain.

In 1964 Arab extremists now sought the removal of British colonial power at the small British protectorate of Aden on the southern tip of Yemen. In areas such as Crater, Khormasker, and Steamer Point terrorist attacks became commonplace. Soldiers found themselves fighting an enemy who simply melted away into the shadows and mixed with the local community. These terrorist groups including the Aden National Liberation Front began attacking UK forces, while north of Aden in the mountains of Yemen, the Quteibi, Ibdali and Bakri tribes joined the fight against the British, particularly in an area known as Radfan. In the spring of 1964, the main Radfan based tribe, backed with Egyptian and Yemeni weapons, mined the Dhala road and began regular ambushes. Their activities provoked a swift response. Paras of B Company 3rd Battalion Parachute Regiment joined 45 Commando RM and the Federal Regular Army, in an operation known as 'Radforce' and set out to dominate the Dhanaba Basin and secure the village of El Naqil. The initial plan called for a night-

Paratroopers search suspected terrorists. (DPL Archives)

Paratroopers of B Company 3rd Battalion operating in Radfan. The regiment was the last British Army unit to leave Aden. (DPL Archives)

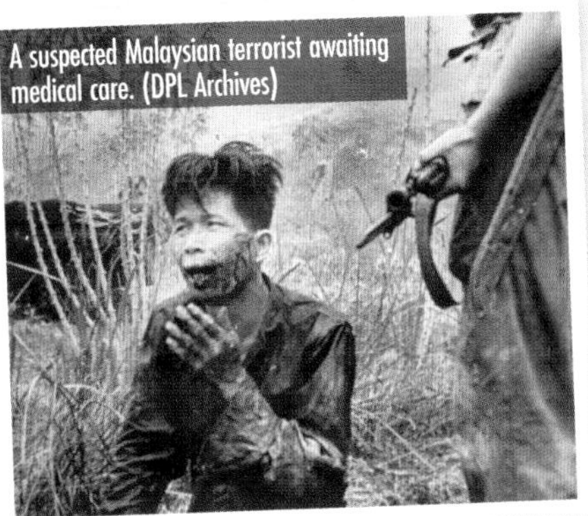
A suspected Malaysian terrorist awaiting medical care. (DPL Archives)

The streets of Crater where British families lived before the insurgency started. (DPL Archives)

time drop by B Company, on a key feature codenamed Cap Badge. But the jump was cancelled and instead they spent 30 exhausting hours marching and fighting to take their target. In recognition of their success, they renamed El Naqil 'Pegasus village' and then along with 45 Commando withdrew to Aden. This was the first of many assaults into the mountains to counter the Arab rebellion. However, by 1967, a large part of British forces in the province had been sent back to the UK, as plans were laid for the eventual withdrawal of British Forces from Aden.

Earlier in 1964, the 2nd Battalion had been sent to Singapore for jungle warfare training, after Indonesia threatened to invade the Malaysian state of Borneo. The remainder of the unit followed in March 1965, and moved direct to the Indonesian border. A month later one of the biggest battles of the war took place, when an Indonesian battalion attacked B Company of 2nd Battalion.

More than 50 Indonesians were killed, the Paras lost two men with seven injured. This short, but intense Far East deployment, ended in July, the battalion having been awarded eight decorations including two Military Medals. In the same year, the 3rd Battalion was sent into Guiana on internal security duties as the country prepared for independence. The next operation for the Paras was to be in 1969, when 2 Para was sent to Anguilla after an armed insurrection on the Caribbean Island. Briefed to expect an opposed landing, there was no resistance and instead the battalion spent six months helping the local community, for which they won the Wilkinson Sword of Peace. ●

Paratroopers spent weeks in the jungles of Malaya on patrol. (DPL Archives)

Paratroopers from the 3rd Battalion Parachute Regiment take shelter in cow sheds near Stanley during the Falklands conflict. (DPL)

The Argentines landed in Port Stanley on April 2, 1982, with Buenos Aires claiming the Falklands was their sovereign territory. (Falkland Islands Govt)

READY FOR

Since 1969 the Parachute Regiment had been deployed in Northern Ireland on internal security operations. Then in early 1982 as the 1st Battalion remained on duty in the street of Belfast, both the 2nd and 3rd Battalions found themselves being recalled from leave and sent 8,000 miles to the South Atlantic as part of a British Task Force after Argentinian forces invaded the Falklands on April 2. Codenamed Operation Corporate, the conflict saw the Paras face some of the bloodiest fighting at Goose Green and Mount Longdon, which was recognised with the award of two Victoria Crosses.

ANYTHING

The 'on-call' battalion was the first to be tasked to head to the Falklands. Cold weather clothing in the form of wind proof smocks, gloves, and Arctic hats had been issued so quickly that many soldiers had not had time to sew their wings and battalion DZ onto the new jackets. The Paras wore the smocks but abandoned the winter hats in favour of their red berets or their special para helmets. The 3rd Battalion joined their green beret cousins of the Royal Marines aboard the liner SS *Canberra*, which had been requisitioned by the Ministry

During the journey to the South Atlantic the Paras took part in daily physical training as well as weapon handling. (DPL Archive)

Paratroopers take part in helicopter training during the trip south to the Falklands. (DPL Archive)

of Defence, for the journey to assault the Falklands beaches . This was to be followed by a battle march across the island to regain sovereignty. Aboard the ship they took part in daily physical and weapon handling training.

Within days the 2nd Battalion was also called up and embarked on the car ferry MV *Norland*. On May 21, the force made an amphibious landing at San Carlos and

Ajax Bay and for the next week air attacks against the beachhead took place daily. On May 26, the 2nd Battalion under the command of Lieutenant Colonel 'H' Jones, was ordered by the brigade commander, Brigadier Julian Thompson, to move south and engage the Argentinian strategic reserve and secure the airfield on the Darwin-Goose Green border. The attack began in the early hours of May 28, with naval and artillery

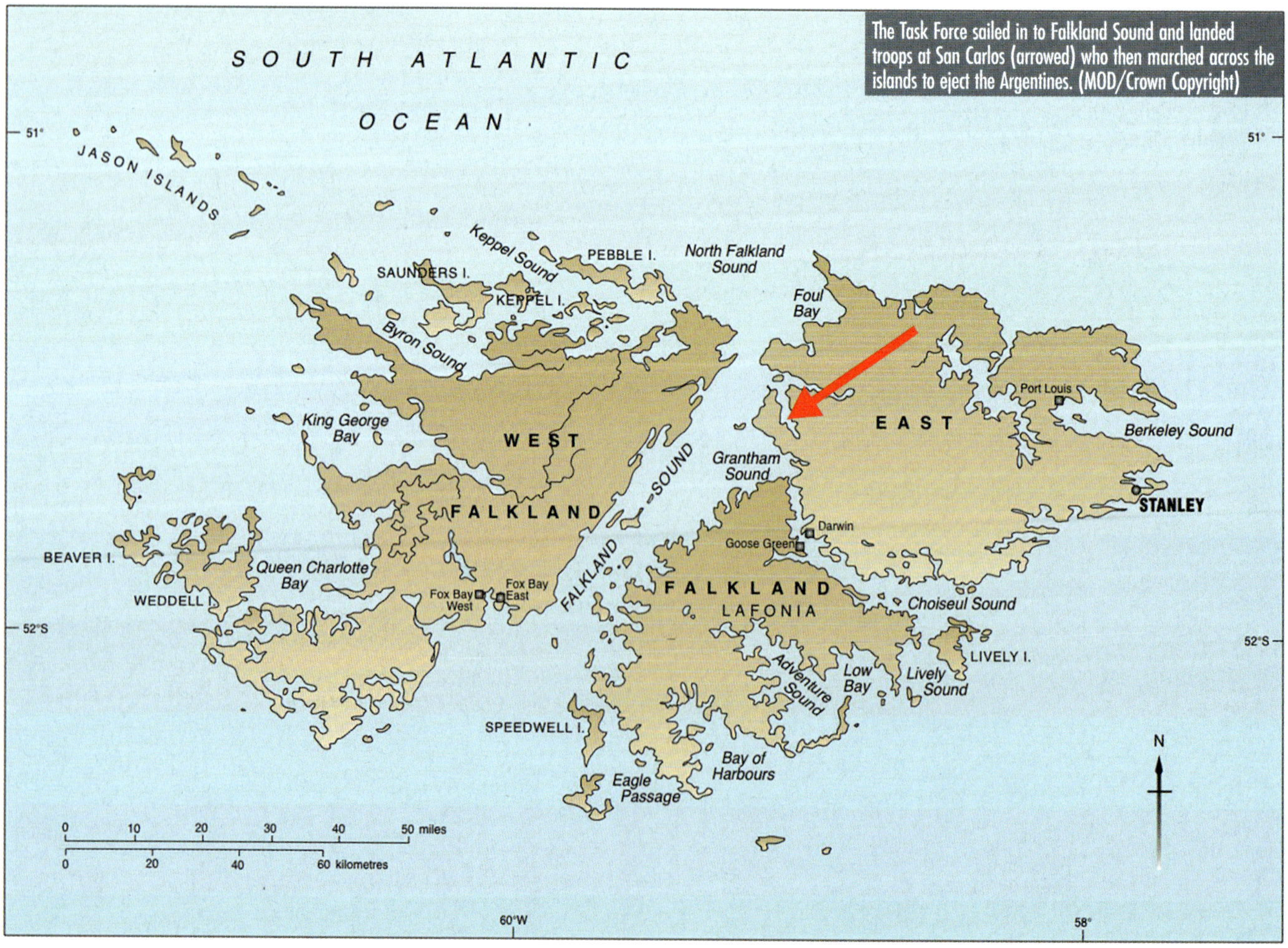

The Task Force sailed in to Falkland Sound and landed troops at San Carlos (arrowed) who then marched across the islands to eject the Argentines. (MOD/Crown Copyright)

The MV *Norland* ferry which carried the 2nd Battalion comes under Argentine attack in San Carlos. (DPL Archive)

support. But by daylight it was clear the enemy's defences were much stronger than reported. In order to get a true picture of what was happening, 'H' Jones went forward himself to ensure that the thrust of his battalion's assault was not lost at this most vital point. Supported by his reconnaissance party, he went further forward and spotted the source of the enemy firepower, which was well dug in and threatening to cause more casualties to his troops. Colonel 'H' seized a machine gun, then charged the enemy position and although hit, continued his charge before being hit again, falling a few feet from the trench he had assaulted. A helicopter piloted by a young Royal Marine officer attempted to fly in to evacuate the wounded colonel, but was shot down in the battle, killing its crew. His courage and leadership

The task force goes ashore by landing craft and helicopter into San Carlos. (DPL Archive)

won Colonel 'H' the Victoria Cross, in what was the Paras first major war-fighting confrontation since 1945.

Battle Honours

Shortly after 'H' Jones was killed, a company group from the 2nd Battalion swept through and attacked the enemy, who quickly surrendered. The Paras had expected a couple of hundred prisoners. Instead, 1,350 Argentines gave themselves up, more than 250 were dead and 140 wounded. The Paras had been fighting at odds three to one against. The battalion had suffered 15 dead and 40 injured. One of the unsung heroes of Goose Green was Major Colin Connor, who, isolated behind enemy lines, relayed vital information back for his colonel's battle plan prior to attacking the

Paratroopers taken ashore by landing craft at San Carlos. (DPL Archive)

Soldiers are briefed before embarking on operations. (DPL Archive)

Paratroopers wait to be picked up by helicopters. (DPL Archive)

airfield. By the time the battalion had moved off Sussex Mountain for Goose Green, he was already stalking the enemy. In freezing conditions and without food or water, Connor crawled five miles to note enemy positions. For 14 hours he lay still as Argentine lookouts scanned the hills for signs of an advance. Finally, disregarding his own safety, he called in an air strike on enemy positions. He survived to become one of the youngest soldiers in the British Army to receive the Military Cross. He said: "I was only doing what I had been trained for. Any man in 2 Para would have done the same." The 3rd Battalion mounted a night attack on Mount Longdon on June 11 and encountered heavy resistance. With bayonets fixed, B Company's No. 4 platoon found themselves advancing under heavy fire. Sergeant Ian McKay and the platoon commander moved forward to see where the fire was coming from. The commander was shot, and Sgt McKay took over and immediately decided the reconnaissance patrol should change role and attack in order to eliminate the enemy.

Argentine prisoners and wounded on the morning following the battle at Goose Green. (DPL Archive)

Taking three men with him, he broke cover and charged the machine gun post, meeting a hail of gunfire. The corporal was seriously wounded, a private killed and another wounded, but McKay continued the attack on his own throwing grenades into the Argentine position. Sergeant McKay died at the point of victory by enemy fire, falling into the bunker he had captured single-handed. His outstanding courage won him the Victoria Cross - the second for the regiment in the Falklands. Following the capture of Mount Longdon, 3 Para's mortars and fire teams supported 2 Para's attack on Wireless Ridge. Later, 2 Para became the first troops to march into Port Stanley. The regiment was awarded two Victoria Crosses (Posthumous) and 68 other decorations as well as four battle honours.

Northern Ireland

Paratroopers arrived in Northern Ireland as peace keepers tasked to restore calm as violence erupted between Catholic and Protestant communities. The welcome

Paratroopers at Goose Green, after the battle. They faced a much larger Argentine force than they had expected. (DPL Archive)

The memorial at Goose Green erected to Lt Col 'H' Jones. (DPL Archive)

A paratrooper mans a General Purpose Machine Gun amid the cold and wet conditions of the Falklands in June 1982. (DPL Archive)

children and two adults into a corner and stood above them using his body as a shield to protect them from the blast. He was fatally injured while seven RUC officers, two British soldiers and 18 civilians were injured in the attack. As he was being removed by ambulance, local thugs jeered. Willetts died after two hours on the operating table at the Royal Victoria Hospital. He was the first soldier in the regiment to be killed in Ulster and he was later posthumously awarded the George Cross.

The built-up estates of Belfast provided plenty of escape routes for IRA attacks and were difficult to patrol. The IRA could throw a blast bomb over a wall, use kids to distract a patrol while they set up an ambush, or launch a mortar attack on a base in broad daylight. Snipers could strike from an overlooking street and then melt into the community. Soldiers mounted vehicle check points with the aim of intercepting terrorists and carried out routine searches in an attempt to crack down on IRA arms caches. But hardline Catholics,

cups of tea were soon replaced with bricks and bottles being thrown at soldiers, as it became evident that the military were trapped in the middle of a sectarian divide - anything they did would be seen by one side as favouring the other. All three battalions of the Parachute Regiment served in the province. However, no one could imagine that this would become the British Army's longest operational campaign. For more than 30 years the Paras were constantly deployed across the Province, on what was codenamed Operation Banner. While the regiment was often accused of being 'too robust' many forget the sacrifice that Sergeant Mick Willetts of 3rd Battalion made in 1971. He was based at Springfield Road Police Station in West Belfast when a man in his mid-twenties emerged from a car and threw a suitcase containing a blast bomb into the lobby of the station. Sgt Willetts thrust two

Casualities at Mount Longdon are prepared to be evacuated by helicopter. (DPL Archive)

Jubilant soldiers of 3rd Battalion the Parachute Regiment after victory at Mount Longdon. (DPL Archive)

The 2nd Battalion was the first to enter Port Stanley. (DPL Archive)

A solider pays his respect to those who died in the 1982 conflict. (MOD/Crown Copyright)

Paratroopers received tea and cakes when they first arrived in Northern Ireland. (DPL Archive)

In the early 1970s riots and bombings were common across Northern Ireland. (DPL Archive)

also known as Nationalists and Republicans, created 'no-go' areas to stop the police and military going into their estates.

The Paras were regarded by commanders as a 'no nonsense' unit and in 1972, despite not being based in Londonderry senior officers sent the Paras in to oversee and police a civil rights march which ended in bloodshed when soldiers shot 14 civilians at what became known as 'Bloody Sunday'. The events resonate more than 50 years later and on December 14, 2023 a judge ruled that a former member of the regiment, who cannot be named, is to stand trial on two counts of murder and five counts of attempted murder. No date for the trial has yet been set.

Two major inquiries blamed the army for a series of operational failures and the Paras became the IRA's most hated unit. Just a month after Bloody Sunday, the IRA bombed the officers' mess of 16th Parachute Brigade in Aldershot, killing seven people. Among the victims were five women, a gardener, and a Catholic padre. But the IRA claimed this was a legitimate target. As the violence continued the IRA launched a bombing campaign and the army were sent into Republican estates to smash the so called 'no-go' areas. A decision was made to intern suspected terrorists, both ➲

A vehicle check point in Belfast at which soldiers checked a driver's identity to try and reduce terror activity. (DPL Archive)

Republican and Loyalists, in a policy that saw hundreds locked up in prison.

In the rural border areas of South Armagh and Fermanagh the Paras were in their element. They were able to restrict the Provisional IRA by deploying covert observation patrols to monitor their activity and reduce their ability to operate. People and more importantly the Provisional IRA never knew where soldiers were, or if they were being watched. The tactic had huge psychological impact and restricted the terrorists' activities, although they remained active. Across the border region helicopters were now being used to support patrols flying teams of soldiers who would mount surprise vehicle check points in remote areas. Based on intelligence, weapons searches were increased, and the army now benefitted from enhanced night-vision systems. The border town of Crossmaglen had become the focal point for the Provisionals. They saw the small market community as the capital of south Armagh and constantly attacked the army. Helicopters were being shot at, police

Republican estates were decorated with colourful murals – soldiers patrolled these states with the Royal Ulster Constabulary. (DPL Archive)

The Parachute Regiment deployed foot patrols with armoured Land Rovers to provide mutual support in areas of west Belfast. (DPL Archive)

A paratrooper from 2nd Battalion on the streets of west Belfast. (DPL Archive)

stations mortared, and command detonated bombs planted to kill soldiers.

In August 1976, the 'Provos' planted a bomb in a bike outside the security base in the town and detonated it as Private James Borucki passed. He was serving with 3 Para and in memory of him the fixed observation post at Crossmaglen was named 'Borucki sanger'. Numerous Provisional names were associated with the murder of the young Para and when 40 Commando relieved the Paras, operations were mounted to detain the culprits. Covert observation operations were now hitting the Provos hard, they did not know where the British Army was, and this induced fear. In Forkhill and Crossmaglen the Provisionals found it hard to operate. Undercover patrols were now regularly deployed in the open countryside, in houses and abandoned properties. For paratroopers deployed on 'covert patrols' in the countryside where they sometimes sat for days the biggest threat remained inquisitive dogs. In a bid to maintain its credibility among the local population the Provisionals stepped up mortar attacks. The success of the military's undercover patrols, later named Covert Observation Teams (COT), hit the Republicans' ability to operate, but they remained a serious threat. Attacks on the police station at Crossmaglen forced commanders ⊃

Paratroopers and Royal Marines on patrol, in the border region of south Armagh. (DPL Archive)

to reinforce the base by encasing it in concrete which earned the site the nickname 'the submarine'.

The Provos campaign against the British Army in the border areas of South Armagh consisted of a bombing and sniper campaign. On August 27, 1979, the Provisional IRA ambushed a combined convoy of soldiers from Parachute Regiment and the Queen's Own Highlanders as they passed the Castle of the Narrow Water at Newry - in total 18 men were killed, 16 of them paratroopers. The terrorists had planted an 800lb bomb in a layby near the castle on the main road which ran parallel to the Newry River, a natural border with the south. After the explosion, the Paras came under fire from across the border. A Gazelle and Wessex helicopters flew into rescue the wounded and as the Wessex was lifting off, a second device was detonated killing more soldiers. This second explosion killed ten Paras and two soldiers from the Queen's Own Highlanders. It was a savage and cowardly attack and the biggest loss of life for the regiment in a single day since World War Two. On the same day, the IRA murdered Lord Mountbatten in his boat, as well as Lady Brabourne, two teenagers and their boatman.

Snipers

By the 1990s the Provos' operation in the border region was heavily restricted as the British Army used increased surveillance and sources within local communities to monitor Republican activity. In a desperate move to fight back the Provisionals' commanders now introduced their own psychological weapon – the sniper. Their plan was to use sniper teams in a bid to restrict the British Army's foot patrols in the border regions, with the primary areas of focus being Crossmaglen and the nearby areas of Culyhanna and Cullaville, as well as Forkhill and Jonesborough. The PIRA acquired

Riot training prior to deployment to Northern Ireland. (DPL Archive)

On patrol in a Protestant area of Belfast where groups remain loyal to the crown. (DPL Archive)

A paratrooper on the streets of Belfast wearing a Dennison smock in 95 pattern camouflage. (DPL Archive)

A soldier serving with the 2nd Battalion wearing a protective visor, these were worn by soldiers who stood in the back of a vehicle in a role known as 'top cover'. (DPL Archive)

a number of .50 calibre M82 sniper rifles with an alleged range of 1,800 metres. The weapons sent a powerful message which was highlighted by the tabloid media who referred to one of the snipers by the nicknames being used in Republican bars at the time - 'Goldfinger' and 'the Terminator'. Signs were erected across the region, warning of IRA sniper operations to add to the impression that snipers were everywhere, but in reality, they weren't. The Paras deployed counter sniper teams, as did other units, and within a couple of years had killed two PIRA snipers.

The accumulated period spent operating in the province for the three parachute battalions amounted to 24 years and six months. The Parachute Regiment received over 40 gallantry awards and 180 honours and commendations in what was the longest campaign in the history of airborne forces. ●

EVACUATION FROM SIERRA LEONE

In 2000, the Parachute Regiment spearheaded an evacuation in Sierra Leone, codenamed Operation Palliser. The Revolutionary United Front (RUF) was locked in a bloody civil war with government forces and had committed barbaric acts of violence, including mutilating civilians to prevent them voting in elections. As they moved towards the capital, Downing Street approved the evacuation amid concerns for the safety of British nationals and diplomats based there. At short notice, paratroopers from the 1st Battalion were ordered to mount a Non-Combatant Evacuation Operation (NEO), flying forward to Senegal before being given approval to start the operation.

Freetown, the capital of Sierra Leone which in 2000 was home to 1.5 million people and under threat of being overrun by the Revolutionary United Front. (Sierra Leone government)

The Paras were flown forward to Senegal by C-130 in readiness to mount an evacuation from Sierra Leone. (MOD/Crown Copyright)

By late April, the rebel forces in Sierra Leone controlled a number of villages and had moved closer to Freetown. On May 6, 2000, they blocked the main road connecting the capital to the international airport at Lungi and announced they would soon capture Freetown - which would make any exit by British nationals almost impossible. Two days earlier, on May 4, UK military commanders had presented a plan to evacuate British nationals caught up in the conflict. The then Prime Minister Tony Blair approved a rapid military intervention as security in Freetown deteriorated. Commanders prepared for a Non-combatant Evacuation Operation (NEO) and alerted the 1st Battalion the Parachute Regiment , drawing additional support from D Company, 2nd Battalion, to be ready for operations. They moved to RAF Brize Norton and awaited the word to fly forward in two RAF C-130 Hercules aircraft to Senegal , from where they mounted the mission.

Arriving at Freetown on May 7, the Paras mounted a Tactical Air-Land Operation (TALO) at Lungi airport and quickly secured the perimeter, establishing an assembly area to fly out evacuees. The arrival of the Paras enabled UK nationals to leave and quickly delivered security and stability around the capital. C Company reinforced the battle-group as did D Company the following day. The Paras had been briefed that they would only be in the country for a short period and deployed with minimum equipment – expecting to oversee the evacuation and fly back to the UK within days. Over the course of a week, British forces evacuated approximately 500 entitled UK passport holders from Sierra Leone—almost 300 of whom left in the first two days of the operation. However, the arrival of the Paras boosted morale in the country, with a number of foreign citizens reassured and opting

RAF Hercules transport planes flew in the Paras and were used to evacuate British nationals. (DPL)

to stay as calm was restored. The operation took on a slower pace after the first two days, but personnel and aircraft remained ready to evacuate any entitled persons who had been unable to reach Freetown earlier and to evacuate the British High Commission if the security situation further deteriorated.

The operation quickly evolved into a peace support operation, the UK government agreeing to support the United Nations in returning wider

The regiment established a base at Lungi airport and deployed patrols by Chinook helicopter. (DPL)

stability across Sierra Leone. High profile patrols were deployed at the port in Freetown and the 1st Battalion pushed out into villages around the airport, where they lived in the jungle. The Paras created a safe corridor around the capital with the aim of forcing the RUF to surrender. The Pathfinder Platoon was the furthest away from the battalion, mounting surveillance on the RUF and collating intelligence on their activity. Then on the night of May 17, a Pathfinder patrol came into contact with a force of around 40 RUF rebels at the village of Lungi Loi, some 14 miles away from the airfield, and a fierce firefight ensued. Elements of Charlie Company were loaded onto the two Chinooks and flown into Lungi Loi to reinforcements the PF Platoon. The Chinooks strafed the jungle with fire from 7.62mm miniguns and inserted C Company including a mortar team, into the area. The company linked up with the Pathfinders as an Army Air Corps Gazelle helicopter flew overhead, spotting for the mortar team who engaged the RUF with high explosive rounds. The Paras were also assisted by Nigerian troops, assigned to the UN, who were tasked to

Paratroopers assist British nationals aboard a C-130 Hercules aircraft. (DPL)

RAF Chinook helicopters pictured at Lungi airport. (DPL)

A former British colony, Sierra Leone sits on the West African coast, close to the equator. It is an area of approximately 27,700 square miles, similar in size to South Carolina or Scotland, and has a population of eight million. It shares its southeastern border with Liberia and the northern half of the nation is surrounded by Guinea. The civil war erupted in 1991 when the RUF, with support from the Liberian dictator Charles Taylor 's National Patriotic Front of Liberia. Taylor wanted the RUF to overthrow the then President Joseph Momoh government and benefit from the country's wealth. The resulting civil war lasted 11 years, enveloping the country in bitter violence and leaving more than 50,000 dead and hundreds left with horrific injuries. During the first year of the war, the RUF took control of large swathes of territory in eastern and southern Sierra Leone, which were rich in diamonds. The government's ineffective response to the RUF and the disruption in government diamond production precipitated a military coup in April 1992, organised by the National Provisional Ruling Council (NPRC). By the end of 1993, the Sierra Leone Army (SLA) had succeeded in pushing the RUF back to the Liberian border, but the rebels recovered, with more weapons supplied from Charles Taylor's administration, and the fighting continued.

Sierra Leone sits on the west African coast and had been subject to rebel fighting with arms smuggled across the Liberian border.

Troops board a Chinook to fly out to remote areas away from Freetown. (DPL)

Paratroopers lived in the remote jungles to ensure that the RUF could not attack Freetown. (DPL)

Paras pictured at Freetown airport with United Nations troops from India in the background. (DPL)

A patrol from 1st Battalion provides security overwatch at the port in Freetown. (DPL)

protect the village's rear approaches. The rebels withdrew from the contact, leaving several dead. There were no British casualties.

The RUF operated in gangs, many clearly under-age and many who appeared to be under the influence of drugs. A new group called the West Side Boys (WSB) now emerged as a potential threat. The WSB had seen fighting in Sierra Leone's civil war and had initially been loyal to the rebels then switched to the side of the government but refused to integrate into the reconstituted Sierra Leone Army. Unemployed, often drunk and under the

Mortar crews deployed their weapons in case they were needed. (DPL)

The RUF were heavily armed and wore a combination of uniforms with self-appointed ranks. (DPL)

influence of drugs, they were a fearsome threat for local people.

They were heavily armed and based themselves in and around the abandoned villages of Magbeni and Gberi Bana on opposite sides of a creek, off the main Rokel river. Deep into the jungle, they were 52 miles inland from Freetown, in a location which offered little access. The Sierra Leone government had adopted a policy of containment to avoid further bloodshed and allowed the WSB to live their isolated lifestyle.

Hostages

By late July, the UK government backed a plan to deploy a British Army regiment on what was termed short term training teams to boost the capability of the Sierra Leone Army. The Royal Irish Regiment followed the Royal Anglian Regiment on what seemed a routine deployment. Then on August 25, a mobile patrol of British soldiers, from the Royal Irish Regiment, was captured by the West Side Boys while returning from a visit to Jordanian peacekeepers. They had turned off the main road and down a track towards the village of Magbeni in the Northern Province of Sierra Leone when the patrol, in two Land Rovers, was stopped and overwhelmed by a large number of WSB carrying former British Army SLRs and a variety of Russian machine guns and rocket propelled grenades.

All 11 were taken prisoner along with their liaison officer from the Sierra Leone Army and transported to Gberi Bana on the opposite side of Rokel Creek. Negotiations quickly secured the release of six of the British soldiers, but it soon became apparent that the WSB wanted to use the remaining five and their SLA colleague to bargain and secure a series of demands. Surveillance of the WSB provided detail on their numbers and routines, as well as the area in which the hostages were being held.

An approach to rescue the soldiers by road was ruled out due to the number of roadblocks on the route to the village and an insertion

A breakaway group called the West Side Boys came to notoriety when they later captured a group of British soldiers from the Royal Irish Regiment. (DPL)

Soldiers in the Sierra Leone jungle where the RUF challenged the Para's presence in a firefight with the Pathfinders. (DPL)

Soldiers gave their rations to local school kids as part of their security and stability reassurance to the local community. (DPL)

Brigadier David Richards briefs paratroopers at Lungi airport after their initial operation. (DPL)

Paratroopers can be seen in the foreground at the height of the battle to rescue the hostages from the Royal Irish Regiment. (DPL)

from Rokel Creek was considered unfeasible due to the sandbanks and powerful currents in the river.

With the clear risk that the soldiers could be killed, a rescue was now ordered. The British had given the WSB a satellite phone to facilitate negotiations and a spokesman, who gave himself the name 'Colonel Cambodia,' spoke at length with the BBC making a series of demands. He wanted the government to recognise the WSB, and their leader the self-appointed Brigadier General Foday Kallay, as a legitimate group. 'Colonel Cambodia' spoke for so long that he depleted the telephone batteries. But his call had been tracked and specialists from the Royal Signals were able to determine the exact position of the handset. As planning for a rescue progressed, it became clear that, given the number of WSB and their separation between two locations, either side of the river, the operation would need additional manpower.

This 'extra capability' would be required to deliver a cordon and a potential deception operation while special forces carried out the rescue. 1 PARA were selected for the task – they had already been to Sierra Leone on the NEO in May; they knew the terrain and were already at high readiness. A Company, 1 PARA, with mortars, heavy machine guns, snipers and

Soldiers carried grenades, flares, and a significant amount of ammunition. (DPL)

RAF crew provided firepower from mini-guns fitted in the Chinooks. (DPL)

Paratroopers clear through the objective where the captured soldiers were held. (DPL)

signallers were selected. Major Matthew Lowe headed the company group, which included new recruits who had only passed out of basic training two weeks earlier. He considered replacing them with more experienced soldiers but assessed that this would undermine morale. On August 31, the 1 PARA group was ordered to move to the Air Mounting Centre (AMC) at South Cerney in Gloucestershire, under the cover story that they were conducting a 'readiness exercise.' Mobile phones were handed in to ensure operational security and the company was briefed on the rescue operation that it would support, as the mission was

Chinooks were used to ferry the Paras into the jungle after soldiers from the Royal Irish Regiment were taken hostage. (DPL)

After the battle to free the members of the Royal Irish Regiment, Paras move the through the secured objective. (DPL)

Paratroopers pack in to a Chinook during the operation to rescue the captured members of the Royal Irish Regiment. (DPL)

being shaped. Then, on September 3, Major Lowe and his planning group flew to Dakar, Senegal, to continue their appreciation of the ground.

A short time later, A Company flew to Dakar and within a day moved forward to Freetown in readiness for their role in the operation. Their move followed increasing fears that the Royal Irish soldiers would be killed. A decision was now made to mount the extraction and an A Company group consisting of 140 soldiers would land in two lifts by Chinook and assault Magbeni. Their orders were clear - to defeat the WSB and destroy their military capabilities . In addition, they were to recover the Royal Irish vehicles and ensure that the WSB in Magbeni

Paras inspect buildings where the West Side Boys held the members of the Royal Irish Regiment. (DPL)

RAF Chinook pilots deploy chaff – anti-missile deflectors, during operations above the Sierra Leone jungle. (DPL)

The vehicles that had been captured by the West Side Boys are recovered and flown back to Freetown. (DPL)

Nigerian soldiers deployed with the United Nations worked in support of the Paras. (DPL)

A paratrooper mans a .50 calibre heavy machine gun at Lungi airport. (DPL)

Paratroopers at a base on the edge of the jungle. (DPL)

The West Side Boys recruited young boys who they armed with AK47s. (DPL)

did not cross the Rokel Creek to interfere with the main rescue operation in Gberi Bana.

Rehearsals were held at a remote Sierra Leone Army camp which allowed the support unit of paratroopers to train for their role. It also allowed the soldiers to acclimatise to the tropical heat, which was so humid that the Paras carried minimal equipment to avoid heat exhaustion.

As the mission was launched, the Paras were dropped near Magbeni on what appeared to be firm terrain but was in fact a swamp. They quickly overcame the obstacle and moved forward to assault the WSB and secure their objective where they came under heavy fire. The Paras cleared the position, located one of the buildings the soldiers had been held in and recovered the vehicles. The advance force flew into the objective aboard two Chinook helicopters, one team roping down and the second landing on the flank. Their role being to eliminate any threat from the WSB at Gberi Bana and rescue the Royal Irish hostage group.

The mission was a textbook success, although one British soldier was killed and several injured in the fighting. At least 30 armed WSB were killed in the firefight and many, including the gang's leader, Foday Kallay, taken prisoner. The Royal Irish Regiment soldiers, who had been held for 17 days, were flown to the Royal Navy support ship RFA *Sir Percivale* for medical checks before being flown back to the UK. At the time, General Sir Charles Guthrie, the Chief of the Defence Staff said: "We didn't want to have to assault. But the hostages had been there for three weeks, and the West Side Boys were threatening to kill them."

Several years later, the Ministry of Defence announced that 1 PARA were to be re-roled as the Special Forces Support Group (SFSG), although maintaining their identity as a battalion of the Parachute Regiment. ●

Paratroopers on a reassurance patrol at the port in Freetown. (DPL)

AFGHANISTAN

The Parachute Regiment was among the first units to deploy to **Afghanistan** following the terrorist attacks on the United States in September 2001- few could have imagined that two decades later they would be among the last to leave. The 2nd Battalion arrived in Kabul just before the end of the year tasked with establishing NATO's initial International Security Assistance Force (ISAF). Later, the regiment was called on to spearhead a 'break in battle' into Helmand in the south of the country and then in 2021 were sent back in to spearhead the biggest evacuation of civilians since World War Two.

In the aftermath of 9/11, intelligence agencies in the United Kingdom warned politicians that Britain's own security was now at risk if Afghanistan was allowed to continue to provide a 'safe haven' for groups such as al-Qaeda. Prime Minister Tony Blair gave the United States his full support and the United Nations Security Council issued Resolution 1368 on September 11, 2001, in which it 'unequivocally condemned in the strongest terms the horrifying terrorist attacks'. In mid-October 2001, 16 Air Assault Brigade and 2nd Battalion the Parachute Regiment were put on standby for operations, although the exact nature of the task had not been defined. By mid-November the Northern Alliance, a group of regional ethic forces opposed to the Taliban, swept south to Kabul, backed by Coalition forces, to clear the Taliban from the city. They seized the city on November 14, with the remaining insurgents fleeing to Kandahar. Within days music, which had been banned by the Taliban under their strict Sharia law, was broadcast on Kabul radio for the first time in five years. Men queued at barbers' shops to have their beards shaved off and children flew kites – banned under the extremists.

The first elements of the 2nd Battalion the Parachute Regiment arrived in Kabul just before the end of the year. Their mission was to assist in the maintenance of security within Kabul in order to support the Interim Authority to create a stable environment in which conditions could return to normality. This meant joint patrols with the local police, engaging in community projects, positively influencing opinion formers, and maintaining a non-aggressive posture – all concepts of peacekeeping which had never been in the Afghan mindset. The city was divided up into security areas by ISAF in conjunction with the Afghan police, and while officially they were seen as positive, it was soon apparent that corruption was endemic. The older population had been used to life under the harsh period of Soviet occupation followed immediately by the authoritarian regime of the Taliban. Alongside the delivery of security an intelligence operation quickly established the social dynamics of the city indicating areas where the Taliban still had

A sniper serving with 2nd Battalion pictured overlooking Kabul during the regiment's first tour of Afghanistan on Operation Fingal in 2001. (Steve Wood/DPL)

A paratrooper armed with a General-Purpose Machine Gun on patrol in the streets of the Afghan capital. (Dil Banerjee/DPL)

support. Lieutenant Colonel James Bashall, the Paras' commanding officer, implemented a hearts and minds campaign across the capital to build relationships with the community and the Afghan National Security Forces (ANSF). B Company were tasked to recruit and train a 600 strong Afghan battalion in order to get local forces on the streets of the city. D Company were initially based in the city centre while C (Bruneval) were located in an abandoned building they quickly named 'Frost Camp' – after the Para's World War Two commander.

Kabul looked like a wasteland; some soldiers described it as looking like the aftermath of Hiroshima. On the streets of Kabul, the

In 2001 as paratroopers deployed to Kabul, they wore berets and were welcomed by local people after their liberation from the Taliban. (Dil Banerjee/(DPL)

The regiment was the first to deploy in Kabul on the International Security and Assistance Force (ISAF) operation. (Dil Banerjee/DPL)

battalion patrolled with local policemen. The Paras wore berets instead of helmets and mixed with the public in a deliberate 'hearts and minds approach'. The community quickly became accustomed to paratroopers on the streets but while children smiled and welcomed the soldiers many adults looked fearful that they were being watched by Taliban collaborators across the city. The deployment had been an overwhelming success, apart from one or two minor incidents, but the regiment had delivered calm, stability and security. The battalion's robust tactical approach had avoided major violence, gained trust, and delivered a template of operational success. Policemen had been trained, services restored, and community engagement achieved. This allowed NATO to encourage additional member nations to deploy troops to the city.

Into Iraq

In 2003 the regiment found itself spearheading the invasion of Iraq with the parachute battalions tasked to secure the oil fields around Basra in the south of the country and then provide ongoing security across the UK area of operations in Baghdad. Then just a couple of years later in 2005, Prime Minister Tony Blair agreed to support the expansion of NATO's (ISAF) security in the south of the country.

Chinook helicopters operated with Apache AH64s as escorts. (Dil Banerjee/DPL)

Children were desperate for fun after years of restricted living under the sharia law enforced by the Taliban. (Dil Banerjee/DPL)

In 2006, the 3rd Battalion arrived in southern Afghanistan as the main manoeuvre battle-group of 16 Air Assault Brigade, known as Task Force Helmand (TFH). Their mission was to facilitate the 'civil effect' plan and with

Paratroopers moved among the population as part of their reassurance policy to deliver stability. (Dil Banerjee/DPL)

The city of Kabul with the airport in the background. (Dil Banerjee/DPL)

local partners to identify projects such as new roads, water wells and schools. The initial atmospherics or human intelligence indicators were welcoming, although soldiers reported a 'tense reception' from the elder members of the community. No doubt this was because the Taliban were watching the Paras. They feared the loss of their criminal narcotics business, which they managed with violence and intimidation.

Within six weeks of 3 Para's arrival the insurgents made their move and attacked. On June 11, the battlegroup lost its first soldier. Captain Jim Philippson, of 7th Parachute Regiment Royal Horse Artillery, was killed after Taliban fighters attacked a patrol near Sangin. The incident took place as he led troops to evacuate two soldiers seriously injured in an earlier engagement. They withdrew under fire after summoning air support from Apache attack helicopters. It was the fourth attack on British troops in Afghanistan in less than a month and fighting was now increasing. Political expectations of a quiet 'peace support mission' had been seriously underestimated. Taliban commanders ordered their fighters ➲

Kabul looked like a wasteland, but traders quickly emerged to sell their wares. (Dil Banerjee/DPL)

Soviet armour littered the city, left behind after the Russian occupation of the country. (Dil Banerjee/DPL)

reinforced 3 Para battlegroup, replaced the Gurkhas and spent more than 107 days in Now Zad, recording 148 attacks.

Then on August 20, a patrol from 1 Platoon deployed from Sangin was deployed into the town Corporal Bryan Budd was leading the forward right section and, as he advanced, he observed three enemy positions to his front. One member of his section was hit in his body armour while Lance Corporal Paul Roberts, the MFC (Mortar Fire Controller) was hit in the shoulder. As Privates Stephen Halton and Andrew Lanaghan moved to pull LCpl Roberts into cover, Lanaghan was hit in the face and arm. Pte Halton continued to extract Roberts and Lanaghan, while Cpl Budd pressed home the attack, but he was fatally wounded. The battalion faced further tragedy when a patrol walked into an unmarked legacy minefield on September 6. Corporal Mark Wright, who had deployed to the area in July, was at a nearby observation post when the mine detonated. Realising that at least one casualty was likely to die before a full mine clearance could be completed, Cpl Wright unhesitatingly led his men into the minefield and directed others to safety, before organising the casualty evacuation. Calmly, he ordered all non-essential personnel to stay out of the minefield. As a helicopter landed nearby a third mine was initiated and seriously injured Wright. The remaining medic

A heavily armed paratrooper pictured in Helmand during the first operation in the region in 2006. (Dil Banerjee/DPL)

to attack local government buildings, known as District Centres. Their intent was clear: they wanted to undermine President Karzai's governance in Kabul and send the message that they were in control of Helmand. UK commanders fought any plans to fix soldiers in the District Centres, but a political decision to deploy soldiers to protect the centres was looming. Finally, the order came from NATO (ISAF) for Brigadier Ed Butler, the force commander, to deploy troops into the DCs across Helmand. It was a policy that quickly became known as the 'platoon house' strategy, but contrary to some reports it was not a plan conceived by 16 Air Assault Brigade Combat Team (16 AABCT). Throughout the remainder of 2006 and the enduring campaign, it remained a highly controversial, some would say disastrous decision, and ultimately left the project to deliver security around Gereshk abandoned. The move into the DCs saw D Company of 2 Gurkha Rifles Regiment (RGR) part of the 3 Para battle group deployed to Now Zad where they manned a position known as ANP Hill. A Company (3 PARA) was despatched into Sangin and C Company to the strategic town of Gereshk, leaving B Company to support operations across the province before subsequently moving to Sangin. Later, a small force from the 2nd Battalion the Royal Regiment of Fusiliers, also part of the

In 2003 the regiment found itself spearheading the UK operation into southern Iraq and was tasked to secure the oilfields. (Dil Banerjee/DPL)

A Pathfinder patrol on the outskirts of the city where hundreds of abandoned Russian tanks were stored. (Dil Banerjee/DPL)

Paratroopers clear compounds during the 2006 deployment in Helmand. (MOD/Crown Copyright)

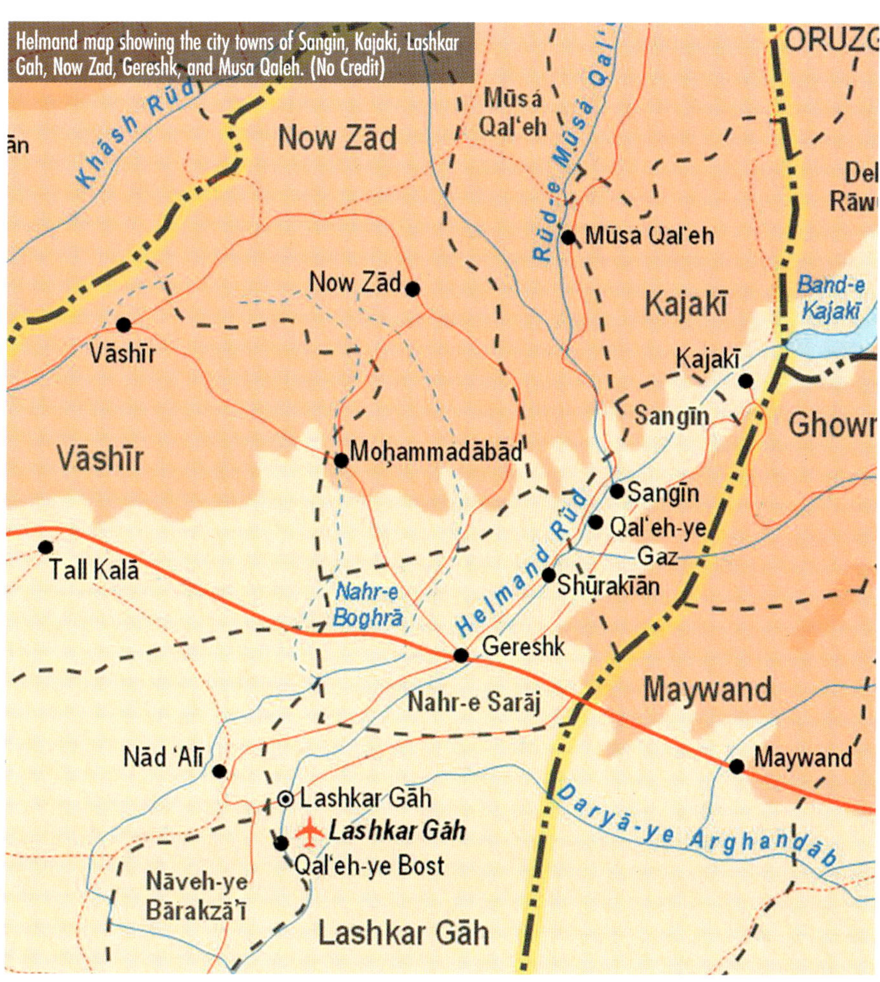
Helmand map showing the city towns of Sangin, Kajaki, Lashkar Gah, Now Zad, Gereshk, and Musa Qaleh. (No Credit)

began treating him but was himself wounded by another mine which caused further injury to Wright and others. Cpl Budd was awarded a posthumous Victoria Cross and Cpl Mark Wright the George Cross. The deployment had been a 'baptism of fire' in which 36 personnel had died in action. The 3rd Battalion battle group had tactically defeated the Taliban on the battlefield, but the enemy remained a threat.

The Parachute Regiment found itself back in southern Afghanistan in 2008 as the UK's involvement evolved into an enduring campaign. The 2nd Battalion faced a series of blistering attacks with C Company, based at Forward Operating Base Gibraltar, near Sangin, involved in daily firefights. In the space of four months Gibraltar was attacked 36 times. In addition, its defenders became embroiled in 29 firefights while on another 22 instances they were either targeted or stumbled across explosive booby traps. The Paras returned to Helmand in 2011 as the UK started to drawdown and end combat operations in southern Afghanistan. From a peak of 137 British bases, only Camp Bastion and Observation Post Sterga 2 remained under British control. Then, on October 26, 2014, the last UK personnel flew out handing over to 215 Corps of the ANA, ending combat operations in southern Afghanistan. But operations were not over, the regiment deployed to Kabul on a security mission dubbed Operation Toral in 2019.

Out of Afghanistan

In August 2021, the Parachute Regiment was put on standby to deploy to Kabul after fears that the Taliban were close to seizing the capital. Within 24 hours of being put on notice to ➲

RAF Chinooks ferry paratroopers across the open desert of Helmand. (MOD/Crown Copyright)

Soldiers wait to be picked up by Chinook helicopter after an operation in Helmand. (MOD/Crown Copyright)

The Army Air Corps Apache AH64 was constantly deployed in support of the Paras. (MOD/Crown Copyright)

Combat Logistics Patrols resupplied the forward operating bases. (Dil Banerjee/DPL)

Paratroopers are airlifted out of the desert by Chinook. (Dil Banerjee/DPL)

Soldiers, wearing new combat clothing and equipped with the Jackal, chat with locals in 2011. (MOD/Crown Copyright)

(CJO) at the military's headquarters in Middlesex now issued an activation order for 16 AABCT to move to Kabul.

On August 12, President Biden agreed to recommendations from his military chiefs to send three battalions of US Marines as well as the 82nd Airborne to bolster security at HKIA and allow an airlift to begin. In London, the UK government came to a similar conclusion and announced that 600 troops would deploy

move, paratroopers from the Air-Manoeuvre Battle-Group - the on-call battalion from the Parachute Regiment - moved to RAF Brize Norton in readiness to fly to Afghanistan. NATO's plan had been for a measured withdrawal of military force. But the pace of departure accelerated after President Joe Biden announced all US troops would be out of Afghanistan by September 11 – the anniversary of the terror attacks on the US mainland. The majority of British and American contractors had also left the country, but thousands of foreign nationals, aid workers and former NATO employees remained. Afghans were now uncertain about the future and large numbers of Afghan soldiers left their units and joined the insurgents. The Taliban now made a move on Kandahar, the country's second major city and the strategically important town of Herat followed. Across the country more Afghan troops surrendered as the insurgents moved closer to Kabul. There was now serious concern that westerners could be in danger. The US, the UK, and many other countries advised their nationals to leave as soon as possible on commercial flights. In the UK, the Ministry of Defence monitored the situation alongside the Foreign Commonwealth and Development Office (FCDO) and contingency plans to repatriate embassy staff and British nationals should the need arise for an evacuation were being reviewed. The Chief of Joint Operations

Operations alongside Afghan Army units increased as the UK prepared to leave Helmand in 2014. (MOD/Crown Copyright)

A hearts and minds operation in central Helmand improved stability and security in 2011. (MOD/Crown Copyright)

to assist in the airlift of UK nationals. Already primed and ready at RAF Brize Norton, the initial elements of 16 AABCT had flown into Kabul. On August 13, the prime minister officially approved the deployment of the Paras to facilitate the evacuation of British personnel from the country. In reality, elements of the Parachute Regiment were already on the ground and working alongside American and Coalition forces to secure the airfield and develop a plan to evacuate nationals.

Later that day the MoD issued a statement saying : "Operation Pitting will be commanded from the UK's PJHQ in Northwood and is the name for military support to the evacuation of British nationals and former British staff eligible for relocation under the Afghan Relocation and Assistance Policy (ARAP). This will be led by the 600 members of the armed forces who have already begun to deploy, with members of 16 Air Assault Brigade leaving this weekend."

In 2021 the Parachute Regiment was deployed to Kabul to oversee an evacuation of UK nationals. (MOD/Crown Copyright)

Paratroopers of the 2nd Battalion arrive in Kabul aboard a C17 in readiness to evacuate UK personnel after fears that the city was about to fall to the Taliban. (MOD/Crown Copyright)

Soldiers outside Kabul airport where thousands of Afghans assembled hoping to get a flight out of the city. (MOD/Crown Copyright)

British and US troops deployed at Kabul airport during the 2021 evacuation. (MOD/Crown Copyright)

Afghans broke through barriers and climbed aboard a US C-17 transport plane. (MOD/Crown Copyright)

Paratroopers recue a child from the huge crowds which packed the airport perimeter.

A paratrooper hands a passport back to an Afghan seeking to escape the city in the wake of the Taliban seizing power.

Afghans desperate for a flight out of the city packed the narrow road around the airport.

Soldiers commandeered vehicles and spray painted them with their regimental name to avoid a 'blue on blue' incident with other forces.

Soldiers patrolled the airport approaches and handed out water and food to waiting Afghans, many of whom slept in the street to avoid losing their place in the queue.

The area at Abbey Gate was so chaotic that barbed wire was laid across the road to try and hold back the crowds and extra troops were drafted in to manage the huge numbers of people hoping to be called forward. Every few hours paratroopers cleared the area in order to allow vehicles to ferry 'entitled persons' (EPs) from the hotel to Abbey Gate and so to a flight.

The evacuation of Kabul, Operation Pitting, marked the end of the UK's 20-year military involvement in Afghanistan in which the Paras had delivered continuous service, The regiment had first arrived in 2001 to serve in Kabul on Operation Fingal. They had been first into Helmand on Operation Herrick and mounted force protection duties on Operation Toral in Kabul. Finally, it was the Parachute Regiment and their supporting units of 16 AABCT who were sent in to provide security and manage the evacuation of the UK nationals in August 2021. The evacuation from Kabul had demonstrated yet again the relevance of the Parachute Regiment's high standard of training. ●

On August 14, the lead elements of the 2nd Battalion were on the ground in Kabul and British passport holders in and around the city were advised to make their way to the Baron Hotel where their 'qualification to be evacuated' was checked before they were escorted across the road to the airfield for processing. The evacuation was focussed on three categories of personnel: British nationals, dual nationals, and those who qualified under the Afghan Resettlement and Assistance Programme (ARAP). Inside the airport UK troops had quickly established a passenger handling facility, which processed all personnel and allocated them a flight to the UK. The area immediately in front of the Baron Hotel was identified as the 'Chevron.' It was a congested area packed with desperate Afghans who waited day and night hoping to escape.

Armed Taliban fighters sit watching British soldiers as Afghans hold up their passports to them.